NOLO *Your Legal Companion*

"In Nolo you can trust." —**THE NEW YORK TIMES**

Whether you have a simple question or a complex problem, turn to us at:

 NOLO.COM

Your all-in-one legal resource

Need quick information about wills, patents, adoptions, starting a business—or anything else that's affected by the law? **Nolo.com** is packed with free articles, legal updates, resources and a complete catalog of our books and software.

NOLO NOW

Make your legal documents online

Creating a legal document has never been easier or more cost-effective! Featuring Nolo's Online Will, as well as online forms for LLC formation, incorporation, divorce, name change—and many more! Check it out at **http://nolonow.nolo.com**.

NOLO'S LAWYER DIRECTORY

Meet your new attorney

If you want advice from a qualified attorney, turn to Nolo's Lawyer Directory—the only directory that lets you see hundreds of in-depth attorney profiles so you can pick the one that's right for you. Find it at **http://lawyers.nolo.com**.

ALWAYS UP TO DATE

Sign up for NOLO'S LEGAL UPDATER

Old law is bad law. We'll email you when we publish an updated edition of this book—sign up for this free service at nolo.com/legalupdater.

Find the latest updates at NOLO.COM

Recognizing that the law can change even before you use this book, we post legal updates during the life of this edition at **nolo.com/updates**.

Is this edition the newest? ASK US!

To make sure that this is the most recent edition available, just give us a call at **800-728-3555**.

(Please note that we cannot offer legal advice.)

1st edition

Nonprofit Meetings, Minutes & Records

How to Run Your Nonprofit Corporation So You Don't Run Into Trouble

By Attorney Anthony Mancuso

FIRST EDITION   AUGUST 2008

Editor   DIANA FITZPATRICK

Cover Design   SUSAN PUTNEY

CD-ROM Preparation   ELLEN BITTER

Proofreading   ROBERT WELLS

Index   SONGBIRD INDEXING

Printing   CONSOLIDATED PRINTERS, INC.

Mancuso, Anthony.
 Nonprofit meetings, minutes & records : how to run your nonprofit corporation so you don't run into trouble / by Anthony Mancuso. -- 1st ed.
    p. cm.
 ISBN-13: 978-1-4133-0892-1 (pbk.)
 ISBN-10: 1-4133-0892-9 (pbk.)
1. Nonprofit organizations--Management. 2. Nonprofit organizations--Law and legislation. I. Title. II. Title: Nonprofit meetings, minutes and records.
 HD62.6.M367 2008
 658.4'56--dc22

                2008012905

Quantity sales: For information on bulk purchases or corporate premium sales, please contact the Special Sales Department. For academic sales or textbook adoptions, ask for Academic Sales. Call 800-955-4775 or write to Nolo, 950 Parker Street, Berkeley, CA 94710.

Acknowledgments

The author thanks Diana Fitzpatrick for editing this first edition. A big thanks to the entire Nolo team for helping me put together and publish another consumer law book for hardworking nonprofits.

About the Author

Anthony Mancuso is a corporations and limited liability company expert. He graduated from Hastings College of the Law in San Francisco, is a member of the California State Bar, writes books and software in the fields of corporate and LLC law, and studies advanced business taxation at Golden Gate University in San Francisco. He has also been a consultant for Silicon Valley EDA (Electronic Design Automation) companies, recently working on a C++ open-source integrated circuit database project team. He is the author of several Nolo books on forming and operating corporations (both profit and nonprofit) and limited liability companies. His titles include *Incorporate Your Business, How to Form a Nonprofit Corporation* (national and California editions), *The Corporate Records Handbook, Form Your Own Limited Liability Company, Your Limited Liability Company: An Operating Manual,* and *LLC or Corporation?* He wrote and programmed *Nolo's LLC Maker* software program, which generates state-by-state articles and other forms for organizing LLCs. His books and software have shown over a quarter of a million businesses and organizations how to form a corporation or LLC. He also is a licensed helicopter pilot and has performed for years as a guitarist in various musical idioms.

Table of Contents

4 The Big Day—Holding Your Meeting

5 Minutes for Directors' Annual and Special Meetings

6 Minutes for Members' Annual and Special Meetings

7 How to Take Action by Written Consent

8 Help Beyond This Book

Appendixes

A How to Use the CD-ROM

B Nonprofit Corporate Contact Information

C Meeting and Minutes Forms

Call, Notice, and Meeting Preparation Forms

Minutes and Consent Forms

Index

Your Nonprofit Meeting Companion

Forming a nonprofit corporation is an intensive, and often exhausting, task. All too often, after the founders successfully create their new entity and obtain tax-exempt status, they take a deep breath and get back to doing what they do best—helping a cause or carrying out a mission. However, when you form a nonprofit corporation, you take on certain responsibilities. Although you probably don't feel like part of a corporation, you must learn how to take action as a corporation and keep proper records. You will need to properly call, notice, hold, and document director, committee, and membership meetings and create a corporate records book to store your minutes and other corporate records.

These are not difficult tasks, but you don't want to neglect them. Failure to take care of your corporate responsibilities could result in your nonprofit being stripped of its corporate and tax-exempt status. This could have disastrous consequences, including the loss of crucial tax benefits for your nonprofit and limited liability protection for your principals. It could also mean that your founders and principals are held personally liable for taxes, penalties, and interest charges assessed by the IRS and state.

This book explains everything you need to know to take care of your basic corporate responsibilities. We show you step by step how to:

- call, notice, hold, and document meetings of directors, members, and committees
- take action by written consent (for directors or members) without a meeting, and
- set up a corporate records book.

We also explain which type of corporate decisions or actions require approval from your directors or members.

The paperwork you need to take corporate action consists of notice and minutes forms for meetings or written consent forms. All the forms you need are on the CD-ROM, so you can quickly and easily make your own customized forms. There are samples of all the forms in the text with detailed instructions on how to fill them out. We also include hard copies of the forms in Appendix C for easy reference.

With this book and its sample forms, you will find that you are able to take care of most of the routine regular and special meeting paperwork for your nonprofit yourself. You may need to consult a lawyer or accountant if you have a complicated legal or tax issue—we explain how to find a helpful nonprofit lawyer and tax adviser in Chapter 8.

The information and forms in this book are intended primarily for nonprofits that are exempt from federal income taxation under Section 501(c)(3) of the Internal Revenue Code. Generally, these are nonprofits that are organized and operated for charitable, religious, education, literary, or scientific purposes. This can include a wide range of nonprofits—from small grassroots organizations to medium-sized and larger institutional nonprofits. Other types of nonprofits (such as 501(c)(4) political lobbying nonprofits, 501(c)(6) social welfare groups, and other mutual benefit corporations—homeowners' associations, social clubs, and the like) may also find this book useful to learn how to hold and document regular and special meetings of directors, committees, and members.

Congratulations! With the help of this book, you can rest assured that you're taking care of your basic corporate house-keeping responsibilities. Soon, you can get back to other important tasks—whether it's saving the sea turtles, running a museum or hospital, or forming a kid's sports group. ●

Housekeeping 101—Understand and Organize Your Records

L et's start by getting acquainted with certain key corporate documents; ones that you'll refer to time and again throughout the life of your nonprofit. These include your articles of incorporation, bylaws, and other organizational documents. They contain your mission statement, the procedures you must follow to operate your nonprofit corporation, and rules to help you maintain your tax-exempt status.

To operate effectively, you'll need to keep your key corporate documents well organized and easily accessible. We'll show you how to set up a corporate records book to help achieve this. Keeping good records is not merely a formality: It can provide crucial documentation in the event of an audit by the Internal Revenue Service (IRS), a lawsuit, or even a disagreement among directors, members, or anyone else about actions taken by your nonprofit.

Why Incorporate a Nonprofit?

Many nonprofits start out as small grassroots organizations, spurred on by the volunteer and part-time energy of just a few people working out of someone's house or office. Under state law, this type of loosely structured arrangement is considered a nonprofit association. It has the advantage of requiring minimal paperwork and it can obtain tax-exempt status using the standard IRS Form 1023 that nonprofit corporations use. However, every member of the nonprofit is personally liable for the claims, debts, and taxes of the organization. So, as a group increases in size and the scope of its work, it often decides to incorporate to protect its founders and members from personal liability for the group's activities. There are other advantages to incorporating but this is often the main reason groups choose to do it.

Your Key Organizational Documents

Getting familiar with your corporate documents is a bit like reading the directions for a new appliance—tedious but essential. For a nonprofit, you'll find that these documents contain many important rules about how you must operate your nonprofit—everything from how to notify people about meetings to the minimum number of directors you must have.

We'll start with the big three: your articles of incorporation, bylaws, and organizational minutes. Then we'll move on to others like your membership roster and consent forms.

Your Primary Corporate Document—Articles of Incorporation

The primary corporate document for every nonprofit corporation is its articles of incorporation. A corporation comes into existence on the date its articles of incorporation are filed with the state corporate filing office. While most states use the term "articles of incorporation," some states refer to this document as the corporation's charter or certificate of incorporation, or by some other name.

Articles of incorporation contain basic structural information, such as the name of the corporation, its registered agent and registered office address, and the corporation's membership structure, if any. Nonprofit corporations also often include essential tax exemption information in their articles, such as their tax-exempt purpose(s), a clause dedicating their assets to another 501(c)(3) nonprofit organization or class of organizations, and other operating restrictions necessary for the nonprofit to obtain tax-exempt status (such as limitations on political lobbying and prohibitions against self-inurement). These provisions often mirror state and federal tax law requirements for nonprofit corporations and are a useful reminder for the nonprofit about the legal restrictions with which it must comply. They also provide the IRS with the assurance it needs to grant tax-exempt status to the corporation.

Some nonprofit corporations include program or other descriptive information in their articles, such as an expanded mission or outreach statement. This information isn't required in the articles and many nonprofits choose to put it in their bylaws instead because it's easier to change bylaws than articles.

If someone helped you incorporate (such as a lawyer, tax adviser, or paralegal), you may have received copies of these documents in a corporate records book or as part of a "corporate kit," which includes a corporate seal (optional under state law) and a fancy corporate records binder. Some lawyers keep their clients' corporate records, assuming they will handle the organization's ongoing corporate work. If that was the case for you, you will need to request a copy of all the corporate documents in your client file. This is your property, so you have a right to receive it.

If you can't locate a copy of your articles of incorporation, write or email your state's corporate filing office (often the corporations division of the secretary of state's office) and request a certified or file-stamped copy. You may be able to order a copy online. Appendix B lists all the state corporate filing offices with their website addresses. The office usually charges a small fee for copying and sending this form to you.

RESOURCE

Where to get help preparing your articles of incorporation. If you haven't yet prepared or filed your articles, there are books and software that can help you. If you want to incorporate in California, see *How to Form a Nonprofit Corporation in California* (Nolo). In other states, see *How to Form a Nonprofit Corporation* (Nolo). Also check your secretary of state's website for sample or ready-to-use forms. You can find the name and website address of the corporate filing office for all 50 states in Appendix B.

Your Operating Manual—Bylaws

The bylaws of a corporation are its second most important document. Bylaws basically serve as a corporation's operating manual. Anytime someone has a question like, "What's the maximum time one of our board members can serve?" they'd look to the bylaws for answers. Bylaws contain the rules and procedures for holding meetings (like call, notice, quorum, meeting, and voting requirements), electing directors, appointing officers, admitting members (for a membership corporation), and taking care of other essential corporate formalities.

You don't file bylaws with the secretary of state—they are an internal document. However, when you apply for tax-exempt status from the IRS, you must include a copy of your bylaws with your federal tax exemption application.

Most state nonprofit statutes have provisions that cover basic corporate governance matters just like your bylaws. But don't worry, you are free to deviate from state law and fashion your own governance rules—as long as the rules you put in your bylaws (or elsewhere) don't conflict with or violate a mandatory state law provision. For example, say your state law requires that at least six people must attend directors' meetings in order to achieve a quorum. (Quorum rules are typical provisions of state laws.) You could set your quorum at eight people, but you couldn't set it at four people, or below the statutory minimum.

Often, nonprofits simply restate the state law requirements in their bylaws. That way, they know that if they follow their bylaws, they are complying with state law. It is also more efficient to have all the important operating rules easily accessible in one document. In any case, if a nonprofit's bylaws don't address an issue covered by state law, the state rules usually kick in.

TIP

Make sure your bylaws are up-to-date. Fortunately, major changes to corporate laws generally only happen every decade or two, when states modernize their corporate statutes. Nevertheless, it's possible that bylaw provisions that were valid at the time you adopted them will later become out-of-date and invalid under new state law provisions. If you plan to take major corporate action (such as restructuring your board or issuing a new class of membership), check your state's current nonprofit corporation act and make sure your bylaws meet the law. We provide the website address for each state's nonprofit corporation act in Appendix B (and see "Checking Other Laws," below).

Bylaws also usually recite important federal or state tax exemption requirements. Again, this ensures that if a nonprofit follows its bylaws, it is doing its best to maintain its tax-exempt status. This information is also necessary to assure the IRS and the state that a nonprofit is eligible for tax-exempt status. Nonprofit bylaws typically include other rules for governance not addressed by state or tax law, such as the composition and operation of advisory committees, the duties of officers, and the rights and responsibilities of informal, nonvoting participants in the organization. These are all useful pieces of organizational history, especially if and when key staff members leave. Some nonprofits choose to give a more detailed description of the group's purpose and programs, expanding on the summary given in the articles.

Make sure you have a copy of your most recent, up-to-date bylaws. If you don't have bylaws yet or want to prepare new ones, there are books that can help you with this task. If your nonprofit corporation was formed in California, see *How to Form a Nonprofit Corporation in California* (Nolo). For help preparing state-specific bylaws for any other state, see *How to Form a Nonprofit Corporation* (Nolo).

Your Personal Liability Protection Can Be Lost: Don't Get Lazy!

If you want the advantages you get as a corporation (including the personal protection of limited liability for your directors, officers, staff, and members), you must follow legal requirements for running it, such as holding and recording meetings, keeping separate books and bank accounts, and following corporate and tax laws. If you don't abide by the rules, you could find your nonprofit stripped of its corporate and tax status—and the benefits of that status, such as:

- **Limited liability.** Corporate directors, officers, staff, and members usually are not personally liable for the debts or claims made against the corporation. This means that if the corporation cannot pay its debts or other financial obligations, creditors cannot seize or sell the personal assets of corporate directors, officers, employees, volunteers, or members.

- **Tax exemption.** A corporation is a separate taxable entity and can obtain tax-exempt status under federal and state law. If a nonprofit loses its tax exemption, it must pay corporate income tax on its net revenue (the corporate tax rate applies to nonexempt nonprofit associations too).

- **Employee benefits.** A person who works for wages for a nonprofit corporation is an employee and qualifies for employee benefits, such as medical reimbursement and insurance, disability insurance and payments, and different types of corporate-sponsored retirement plans. (However, a tax-exempt nonprofit cannot set up profit-sharing or other equity-sharing plans.)

- **Other benefits.** Tax-exempt nonprofit corporations can qualify for grants, reduced mailing rates, real and personal property tax exemptions, and other benefits available only to recognized 501(c)(3) organizations.

- **Perpetual existence.** A corporation has an independent legal existence that continues despite changes in directors, management, or the nonprofit mission or program.

> **TIP**
>
> **Whenever you have a choice, put material in your bylaws instead of in your articles.** Many states' laws allow corporations to put their operating rules and procedures in their articles of incorporation or bylaws. If you have a choice, it's usually better to put the material in your bylaws— they're easier to change than articles. The voting requirements to amend bylaws are generally less stringent and you most likely don't need to file anything with the state. Amending articles often requires a higher vote and you must file a formal amendment with your state's corporate filing office.

Your First Meeting—Organizational Meeting Minutes

The first order of business for most newly formed nonprofit corporations is to hold a meeting to approve standard items of business necessary for starting operations. It's usually referred to as the organizational meeting of the corporation. The meeting can be held by either the board of directors or the incorporators— whoever signed and filed the articles on behalf of the corporation (sometimes a lawyer or paralegal).

The minutes of this meeting are simply a formal record of the proceedings and actions taken. Typically, these actions include such items as:

- tax elections—for example, setting your accounting period and tax year. Nonprofits often choose a calendar tax year and accounting period, which ends on December 31.
- for a membership nonprofit, approval of the issuance of memberships, membership certificates, and, if applicable, the setting and scheduling of membership dues or assessments
- approval of the bylaws
- appointment of officers
- authorization for and establishment of the board and other committees

- authorization to apply for tax-exempt status or, if that's already been taken care of, a statement of the effective date and terms of the organization's tax exemptions, and
- approval of other beginning transactions of the corporation, such as the opening of a corporate bank account, approval of leases, hiring or staffing resolutions, and the like.

The meeting minutes also may include reports and recommendations presented by organizational committees and initial staff members.

You should keep copies of these reports and records of any discussion attached to the organizational minutes in your corporate records book. Having a record of this information may be essential for your group to make informed decisions later.

> **TIP**
>
> **Lost your first minutes already?** Some nonprofit corporations—especially those created in a rush—don't have minutes of the first meeting of the board of directors or incorporators. It's not the end of the world; you can proceed without them or recreate them. But be sure to note in your recreated minutes that they were created after the fact to memorialize actions taken by your initial board or incorporators at their first meeting.

Membership Roster

If your nonprofit is a formal membership organization, you will need to keep a roster of members, with each member's name, address, and contact information (phone number, email, and physical address). (Not sure whether you're a membership organization? See "What Is a Membership Nonprofit?" below). It's a good idea to record other relevant information for each member, such as the date a member joins or leaves the membership, dues paid, volunteer hours served, and so on. The membership roster helps track members and their activities, and verify their participation in the group's program.

If you have a membership nonprofit and haven't set up a membership roster, do so right away. We have included a Membership Roster form on the CD-ROM that you can fill in and update as needed. Keep a hard copy record of your current roster in your corporate records binder.

What Is a Membership Nonprofit?

No matter how many enthusiastic supporters your nonprofit has, you may not be, technically speaking, a "membership nonprofit." In fact, you might not want to be. In most states, a "member" has a special definition under the law, and includes people who are given the right to vote for directors in the corporation's articles or bylaws. The law may give members additional rights, such as the right to vote on structural changes to the nonprofit, transfers or sales of corporate assets, and whether to dissolve the nonprofit. In most states, a member also has the right to contest being expelled from the nonprofit, plus certain due process rights in the event of a termination.

Nonprofits can establish a membership structure for their organization in their articles or bylaws. If your organization doesn't, the directors fill vacancies on the board and approve corporate action. Most small nonprofits choose not to establish a formal membership because it's simpler to have only the directors involved in managing the organization.

And just to be clear, this formal membership structure shouldn't be confused with the informal type of membership that nonprofits often create for their supporters, patrons, contributors, and advisors. These informal members have no rights under state law to participate in a nonprofit's affairs. Whenever we talk about members in this book, we are referring to the formal type of member and membership structure.

Ongoing Records—Minutes and Written Consents

Whether your nonprofit is just starting up or you've been in existence for awhile, think "paper trail." You should keep minutes of all regular meetings of your board or members, as well as minutes of special meetings and records of actions taken by written consent.

These minutes and written consents are an important record of corporate decisions and actions (great protection against faulty memories), and can provide crucial evidence that your group acted responsibly and with proper authority if disputes arise later. No matter how congenial your meetings are, you could come up against tough or probing questions from members, directors, contributors, creditors, the IRS, or anyone else. And as time passes, even people involved in the decision making may forget why, for example, you agreed to close down a certain program or who was involved in firing the executive director. No organization is immune from controversy and dissension.

Written minutes and resolutions that record important decisions and the votes taken to approve them can help defuse potential blowups within the organization and avoid problems with outsiders. You should keep all these records in your corporate records book with your other key corporate documents.

Other Records

Your nonprofit may already have amassed a pile of other records, including contracts, tax exemption applications and related correspondence, leases, promissory notes, and other legal forms or paperwork. Make copies of these documents and keep them in your corporate records book. If someone handled the work for you, such as a volunteer lawyer or tax adviser on your board, ask the person to give you copies of any records.

Organize Your Corporate Records

If you have not done so already, you should set up a corporate records book to store all your key documents. You can do this on your own with a three-ring binder or you can use a customized corporate kit designed for this purpose (available from stationery stores or online from a corporate forms provider). Your corporate records book should contain:

- your articles of incorporation
- your bylaws
- minutes of your organizational meeting (or first directors' meeting)
- a list of the names and addresses of your directors
- for a membership organization, a membership roster listing the names and addresses of your current members and membership certificates and stubs (although these are not required and most nonprofits do not issue certificates)
- minutes of all annual and special meetings of directors and members (if any), and
- written consents to any actions taken by the board or members.

Keep your corporate records book at the principal office of your corporation so you always know where to find it. As we mentioned earlier, you'll refer to these documents time and again. You'll use them on an ongoing basis to check rules and procedures for running your organization—what constitutes a quorum; who can call a meeting; what is proper notice; and so on.

Keeping your documents well organized and accessible will help you operate more effectively. When procedural or corporate governance questions come up, you'll be able to check quickly, answer with confidence, and move on. That way, you can stay focused on the more interesting and important program-related work you do. Having your documents in order can also help in the event your group is ever involved in an IRS or financial audit or a dispute among directors, members, creditors, contributors, or anyone else.

Looking Up the Law Yourself

In addition to the rules and procedures contained in your articles and bylaws, each state has a good-sized pile of laws that govern the organization and operation of local nonprofits. Some of these rules will be restated in your bylaws, but there will undoubtedly be times when you'll need to look up the actual law yourself. Although you may not be champing at the bit to read a corporate statute, it's not as hard as sounds. And, more importantly, most small nonprofits can't afford to pay a lawyer upwards of $300 per hour every time they have a legal question or need help handling a legal matter, particularly something related to ongoing corporate formalities and straightforward procedures.

We'll teach you basic skills so that you can learn to answer some questions yourself, without having to seek, and pay handsomely for, outside legal assistance. We also encourage you to find a lawyer who is willing to provide some backup services as a legal coach rather than a full-fledged legal representative (see Chapter 8).

Locating Your State's Nonprofit Laws

State nonprofit laws are often designated as the Nonprofit Corporation Act or by some similar name. The easiest way to find them is to look online, using the Web addresses we provide in Appendix B (look for your state's "Nonprofit Corporation Act"). If you want to look up the law the old fashioned way (in a book), the county law libraries in most states are open to the public. Don't hesitate to ask for assistance—research librarians are usually available.

The Model Revised Nonprofit Corporation Act

The nonprofit corporate statutes of many states contain the same, or quite similar, rules for organizing and operating business corporations. One reason for this uniformity is that a number of states have adopted some, most, or all of the provisions of a standard law called the Revised Model Nonprofit Corporation Act.

The following states have enacted a substantial portion of the provisions of the Revised Model Nonprofit Corporation Act:

Arkansas	Montana	Tennessee
Indiana	North Carolina	Washington
Mississippi	South Carolina	Wyoming

Approximately half of the states have adopted selected provisions from the Act. To browse the Act online, go to: www.paperglyphs.com/nporegulation/documents/model_npo_corp_act.html.

Finding Answers to Your Questions

Once you have found your state nonprofit law, it's often quite simple to find answers to questions you have. You can browse through the table of contents at the beginning of the act or look for a mini table of contents at the beginning of each section heading. Each heading should cover a major area of corporate operation or procedure, such as formation, meetings, directors, members, officers, or records and reports. Major headings are further broken down into subheadings that deal with specific matters within that section, such as articles of incorporation and bylaws, or director meetings and membership meetings. If you are searching online, you can also usually search for the subject you're interested in by entering a few key terms, such as directors' meeting or notice.

Checking Other Laws

In addition to a state's nonprofit laws, there are other laws that regulate specific areas of corporate or nonprofit activity. These include:

Federal Tax Code. The Internal Revenue Code, particularly Section 501(c)(3), and Internal Revenue regulations, are the primary sources of information about the tax requirements for forming and operating a tax-exempt nonprofit. However, these laws and regulations are incredibly arcane and difficult to parse and understand, even for a practiced professional. This is not light reading. You can find the Internal Revenue Code online at http://benefitslink.com/taxcode/index.html and the Code of Federal Regulations at www.access.gpo.gov/cgi-bin/cfrassemble. cgi?title=200626.

State Tax or Revenue Code. If a state imposes a corporate income or franchise tax, the state's tax or revenue code will typically contain these provisions as well as the rules that apply to obtaining an exemption from state corporate or franchise taxes.

Commercial Code. The state's commercial code contains the rules for entering into and enforcing commercial contracts, promissory notes, and other standard commercial documents.

Civil Code. The state's civil code may contain the state's rules related to the regulation of charitable solicitations in your state. In some states, these rules may be part of another law, such as the state nonprofit corporation law or a separate state charitable solicitations law.

Other state and local laws. State licensing and professional codes apply to special types of nonprofits, such as the professional licensing and practice statutes that apply to a nonprofit hospital and the state education code that applies to a nonprofit school. Various state and local laws may impact the activities and operations of all organizations, whether or not they are incorporated, such as state and local building codes.

State Corporate Filing Offices

Even after you've created your nonprofit, most states require nonprofits to file periodic reports or statements with the secretary of state or the department of state. There is often a corporations division or corporations department within that office that handles the filings. We provide the name and website address for each of the 50 state offices that handle corporate filings in Appendix B. Throughout this book, we refer to the office that accepts corporate filings as the secretary of state or state filing office, even though in some states this office goes by a different name. If the website address for your state has changed, you can find a current listing of all state government websites at www.statelocalgov.net.

Most secretary of state websites allow you to download corporate statutory forms (articles of incorporation, change of registered agent or registered office address, and so on). Many of these state websites also contain links to your state's corporate tax office and state employment, real property tax, licensing, and other agencies.

> **TIP**
>
> **Check your state's tax office website.** The state tax office is one of the first places you should look to make sure you understand and are in compliance with your state's tax exemption rules and annual filing requirements. In most states with a state corporate income tax, once you obtain your federal tax exemption, you also qualify for a state income tax exemption for your nonprofit. But even when this is true, you will need to comply with your state's annual tax-exempt nonprofit information tax return requirements.

When to Consult a Professional

Holding corporate meetings and preparing standard resolutions and other bits of paperwork are usually routine tasks for corporations. However, if the decision you are facing is complex, you anticipate any complications or objections, or you simply have questions and need more information, consult with a tax or legal specialist before using the forms in this book. A consultation of this sort will be far more cost-effective than making the wrong decision and having to fix it later. For information on choosing or using a legal or tax adviser, see Chapter 8. ●

Obtaining Board or Member Approval—Meetings and Written Consents

n this chapter, we discuss when you need to obtain board or membership approval for your nonprofit's actions and the different ways you can get it. Not every decision requires formal corporate action or approval by the board—day-to-day operational matters are usually handled by staff without board involvement. However, board approval is required for the organization's most important actions and decisions, so you'll need to know when and how your board (or, in some cases, your members) can take action and how to properly document those decisions or actions.

When Is Board Approval Required?

Your board of directors is the primary decision maker for your nonprofit and is responsible for overseeing its management. As a result, your board should approve any decision involving significant financial, legal, or tax issues or any major program-related matter.

Some of the most common legal and business matters that nonprofit boards approve are:

- amendments to the articles of incorporation or bylaws
- the issuance of classes of memberships, setting membership dues, special membership assessments
- the hiring and firing of the executive director and other key officers and staff
- salaries and fringe benefits for officers and key employees
- the purchase of commercial or director and officer liability insurance; indemnification for directors and officers
- real estate construction, or the lease, purchase, or sale of real estate
- the appointment of key officers and departmental managers, and
- the terms of loans and other obligations the nonprofit takes on.

In addition to these legal and business matters, much of a board's time is spent on issues related to the group's mission and its funding or financial health. Generally, the board is responsible for overseeing the organization's fundraising program, its grant outreach efforts, financial accountability practices and procedures, and financial audits. Often a committee of the board, or an independent committee, initially handles the financial and program-related business. The committee then presents its findings and recommendations to the board for a vote by the full board. Both the committee meetings and the board meetings should be documented with minutes and any committee reports should be attached to the meeting minutes and kept in the corporate records book.

Luckily, you don't need to obtain board approval or keep documentation for every decision or action by your organization. Routine operational matters, such as administrative staff procedures, can be handled by staff without board approval. For example, the board may approve the fundraising goals for the year, but the staff can be in charge of the fundraising events and writing and sending out solicitation and thank-you letters. And, if there's no board input or involvement in a matter, there's no need to clutter up your corporate records book with documentation about it.

When Is Membership Approval (or Ratification) Required?

In a formal membership nonprofit, the members are responsible for electing the board of directors. This is usually done at an annual members' meeting. Other than that, members are generally less involved in corporate decisions than the board. Bylaws or state laws usually specify the corporate decisions that members have a right to vote on. You don't always have to ask members to independently consider and approve a matter. In some cases, they are simply asked to ratify a board decision.

The types of decisions that members might have the right to approve or ratify usually relate to structural changes to the corporation or changes to members' rights or responsibilities, including:

- electing the board of directors
- ratifying amendments to articles
- approving changes in the rights, privileges, or preferences of members
- approving the sale of substantial corporate assets, and
- agreeing to dissolve the corporation.

> **TIP**
>
> **Member voting rights apply only to formal members who are given the right to vote for directors in the corporation's articles or bylaws.** Your nonprofit structure may include other types of nonvoting "members" or participants in your program, such as donors, sponsors, contributors, and the like. These individuals have no right to say "yea" or "nay" to any corporate decision. The best way to check the voting status of any person who participates in your nonprofit is to check your bylaws.

How Boards (and Members) Take Action

There are two different ways for a nonprofit corporation to take action and make decisions. You can hold a meeting of your directors or members and vote, or your directors or members can sign written consents without attending a meeting. If the board or members meet, written minutes of the meeting serve as the documentation for the action taken. If the action is by written consent, the written consents are the formal documentation.

Both methods have the same legal result—the board or members' decision is binding and final as long as it was properly done. However, there are situations where it can make more sense to use one method or the other.

Most Nonprofits Prefer Real Meetings

A real meeting allows the board or members to engage in face-to-face discussion and arrive at decisions after debate, argument, or conversation. Most nonprofits favor this method because defining and implementing a nonprofit's program works best through open discussion and consensus-building among the interested parties.

Also, if an issue is significant enough to require board input or approval, it's usually also important enough to warrant an in-person meeting. Directors and members—particularly in smaller nonprofits—often prefer to meet and vote on items of business, particularly if they involve anything significant or controversial. Because of this, many nonprofits make most or all of their decisions at a meeting.

During or after the meeting, the secretary prepares written minutes that show the date, time, place, and purpose for the meeting and the decisions (resolutions) approved by the board of directors or members.

Holding a Meeting in Cyberspace

If you can't get everyone together at the same physical location for a meeting, some or all of your meeting participants can communicate and be "present" electronically instead of in person. As long as all of the meeting participants can hear one another simultaneously, most state laws allow this type of meeting and anyone participating electronically counts as present for quorum purposes.

There are a number of ways that people can simultaneously communicate electronically—from something as simple as a telephone or video (webcam) conference call to a computer conference intranet or Internet hookup using net-meeting software. It can be very useful for boards where it's difficult to get everyone together in the same location.

When Written Consents Make Sense

The written consent procedure is the quickest way to approve and document a formal decision by the nonprofit's board or members. You avoid having to call, give notice of, and hold a meeting. And no one has to prepare minutes of the meeting. Instead, you circulate a written resolution that states the action or business under consideration among the board or members, and those who approve the resolution sign the form.

Written consents work best to handle noncontroversial or routine items of business, such as the approval of a bank authorization form or the extension of a lease. They are also useful if something is needed in a hurry and there's not time to hold a meeting. The only documentation is the written consents themselves, which should be kept in the corporate records book.

How Often Should Your Board or Members Meet?

Annual Meetings. Corporate statutes and nonprofit bylaws often require, at a minimum, annual board of directors' and members' meetings. With a membership nonprofit, the annual directors' meeting often is held on the same day as or shortly after the annual members' meeting. At the annual members' meeting, the members elect the new board; and at the annual directors' meeting, the directors accept their election to the board and transact any additional business brought before the meeting.

> **EXAMPLE:** All officers, directors, and members attend the annual members' meeting of World Vision, Inc. The corporate president and treasurer give reports summarizing nonprofit program, fundraising, and financial operations results of the preceding year and outlining plans for the upcoming year. The members reelect the current five-person board for another one-year term. Next, the members leave, and

the newly constituted board stays behind. First, the board members accept their reelection to the board; then they discuss business plans for the upcoming year.

Routine items of business that typically are dealt with at the annual directors' meeting include the appointment of new officers or committees, the announcement of officer staff salary levels for the upcoming year, and reports of past operations and proposals for upcoming programs or initiatives.

Many nonprofits schedule regular monthly meetings for their board of directors. Meeting annually usually isn't enough for the board to stay in touch with what's happening at the organization. At these monthly meetings, the board will discuss and approve program- and staff-related issues that come up throughout the year. Smaller or less active organizations may schedule regular board meetings less frequently—on a quarterly, semiannual, or even annual basis. If an important item of business comes up between scheduled meetings, the directors can call a special meeting or take action by written consent.

Members are another matter: It's more common for them to meet only annually. Their primary role is, after all, to elect the directors, who are then in charge of overseeing the organization's activities. Sometimes, directors' terms are for longer than one year, in which case member meetings may occur less frequently. Or, if the board is divided (classified) into groups, the members may elect only a portion of the board at each annual members' meeting. Groups with an active membership sometimes schedule more frequent regular meetings or call special meetings to keep their members informed about and engaged in the group's activities.

Special Meetings. All other meetings of the board or members are special meetings, which may be called any time during the year according to the rules contained in the group's bylaws. Nonprofits call special meetings to discuss important items of business that come up between scheduled meetings or to approve legal or tax issues that arise from time to time. For example, a special meeting might be called to approve taking out a loan to buy a van for your outreach program, or buying or leasing new office space. Special membership meetings are held less often, and normally occur only when a special matter is brought by the board before the membership for approval.

It's best to hold all board and member meetings "by the book"—that is, "by-the-bylaws." You should properly call, notice, and hold all meetings and make sure that someone is responsible for taking minutes at each meeting and that the minutes are placed in the corporate records.

How Small Nonprofits Meet

In a small nonprofit, annual meetings of directors and members are held mostly as a formality. At the annual members' meeting, the board of directors is usually reelected, en masse, to a new term (usually one year). At the annual directors' meeting, each director routinely accepts office for the upcoming year—until, of course, the group needs to replace or add new directors.

CAUTION

Check your bylaws for the legal rules. The legal rules and procedures for holding meetings or obtaining the written consents of your directors or members—covering things like notice and quorum requirements—should be in your bylaws. (If you can't find your bylaws, or you're not sure they are current, follow the suggestions in "Organize Your Corporate Records" in Chapter 1.)

Why You Need to Document Key Corporate Decisions

Why bother to prepare minutes of meetings or written consents for important corporate decisions? Here are a few excellent reasons:

- Annual meetings are usually required by state law. If you ignore this requirement, you may lose the limited liability protection of your corporate status.

- Minutes of meetings and other decision-related paperwork provide a record of important corporate transactions. This paper trail can be important if disputes arise. Documentation can later show your directors, members, lenders, contributors, the IRS, and the courts that you acted responsibly and in compliance with applicable laws, regulations, and other legal and tax requirements.

- Sharing or providing ongoing access to your paper trail of key corporate decision making is a good way of keeping members informed of and engaged in your nonprofit's mission. With the media and others ever-vigilant about nonprofit abuses, it's best to be as transparent as possible.

- Directors of small nonprofits sometimes must approve transactions in which they may have a financial interest. Your minutes or consent forms can prove these decisions were arrived at fairly, and in compliance with applicable state law and federal tax-exemption conflict of interest statutes and guidelines. For example, as required under many state statutes, you can show in your minutes that a decision was approved by a majority of directors without counting the vote of interested directors.

- Banks, trusts, escrow and title companies, property management companies, and other institutions often ask corporations to submit a copy of a board or membership resolution as part a loan or property transaction. ●

Premeeting Steps—How to Call, Notice, and Prepare for Your Meeting

S pontaneity and last-minute impulses won't get you very far when planning nonprofit meetings. Before you hold a meeting of your directors, members, or a committee, you'll need to call and provide notice according to the rules in your bylaws and in your state's corporation statutes. What if you don't? You could end up wasting everyone's meeting time, or worse—the actions taken during the meeting could later be contested by other directors or members.

In this chapter, we go through the premeeting steps you must take to properly hold a meeting and also discuss practical measures to get the most out of your meetings.

Premeeting Steps—An Overview

Before you dive into the mechanics of how to prepare for a meeting, here's an overview of the steps you must take to properly call, notice, and prepare for a meeting of your board, a committee, or members:

- Someone calls (requests) a meeting. The person who does so must be authorized under your organization's bylaws or your state's law.
- Someone (most likely the chair of the board) sends notice of the time, place, and purpose for the meeting to directors, committee participants, or members, together with any written materials.
- The meeting is held; business is discussed and approved by directors, committee, or members.
- The secretary prepares minutes of the meeting, which are signed by the secretary, and placed in the corporate records book (either at or after the meeting).

Don't be daunted by the comprehensive list of premeeting steps described below; only a few of them are legally required. Also, don't worry that you'll miss an important step—the minutes forms in the next two chapters remind you to take care of all legally required steps as you prepare those forms.

Board Committees and Advisory Committees May Not Follow the Same Rules

Much of the busywork of nonprofits is handled by committees (usually set up in the bylaws or created ad hoc by the board). But not all committees face the same legal requirements.

These committees can be set up in the bylaws or created ad hoc by the board.

Nonprofit statutes contain special rules for certain board committees, typically called "committees of the board." We call them "board committees." These normally are defined as committees comprised of at least two board members plus other individuals. Under standard state statutes, board committees can make the same types of decisions and approve the same types of transactions as the full board, except certain actions such as:

- approving or recommending to members the dissolution, merger, or the sale, pledge, or transfer of all or substantially all of the corporation's assets
- electing, appointing, or removing directors or filling vacancies on the board or on any of its committees, or
- adopting, amending, or repealing the articles or bylaws.

The state legal rules for calling, noticing, and holding board committee meetings are generally the same as those that apply for special board meetings. Your bylaws, too, may have applied the same rules to both.

Nonprofit boards often appoint another type of committee that serves in an advisory-only role. These committees may have just one or no directors, do not have the authority to act on behalf of the board, and are not regulated by state law. We refer to this type of committee as an "advisory committee" (or simply as a "committee") throughout this book.

Generally, state law is silent as to the rules for calling, noticing, and holding advisory committee meetings. However, many nonprofits put rules about advisory committees in their bylaws—including their names, duties, and the procedures they should follow. Check your bylaws to find out how to call, notice, and hold advisory committee meetings, as well as how to document what happened at the meetings and present this to the full board. If you don't have any rules about advisory committees in your bylaws, we recommend you follow the call and notice rules for board committees.

Going Through the Steps

Below are the steps you should take to prepare for a meeting of directors, a committee, or members. Some of these steps will be required by your bylaws or state law. Others are optional—but will help you get organized and prepare for your meeting, plus provide useful documentation in case of eventual disputes or an IRS audit.

Step 1. Prepare Meeting Folders

You may be surprised at the number of forms and other paperwork that even the most routine meeting can generate. Set aside a blank file folder for each upcoming meeting. Put the date and type of meeting on the tab for the folder—for example, "Annual Directors' Meeting, July 2010" or "Compensation Committee Meeting, March 15, 2010"—and keep the folder handy.

As you create each document for your meeting, place it in this file folder. After the meeting is over and you have prepared and completed all the paperwork, you can transfer the entire contents of the file folder into the minutes section of your corporate records book. You can create the same type of files on your computer to organize your meeting documents. For example, you may wish to create a directory named "Director Mtg 2010" on the hard disk to hold all computer files for the annual 2010 meeting of directors. After the meeting, when all the documents are finalized, be sure to place hard copies of all the final documents from the meeting in your corporate records binder.

Step 2. Use Meeting Summary Sheets

To keep track of key dates and times, including when notices were or should be sent, use the Meeting Summary Sheet on the enclosed CD-ROM (a copy of the form is also in Appendix C). This form lets you enter information summarizing what you've done and when you did it. If questions come up later, these summaries serve as an excellent record of the meetings and as documentation that the meetings were called, noticed, and held properly. Use your Meeting Summary Sheet both as a scheduler and reminder sheet for each meeting you hold.

The Meeting Summary Sheet has room for you to insert general information on the basic call and notice requirements for meetings. Filling in this information should help remind you of the important notice requirements as you plan your yearly list of meetings.

The secretary (or board chair or other person who will call or provide notice for your meetings) should keep Meeting Summary Sheets handy and refer to them often. That way the secretary can keep track of upcoming meetings, and can make revisions and additions to the sheets as necessary. When and if a director, officer, member, or other authorized person calls for a directors' committee, or members' meeting, the secretary should create a new Meeting Summary Sheet and fill in all relevant information.

TIP

Meeting Summary Sheets can help if your organization is audited. They'll come in handy if you later need to show insiders, outsiders (including the IRS and others), at a glance, that you paid attention to the separate legal existence of your nonprofit by holding meetings in accordance with your bylaws and state law. Summaries of this sort are often prepared by lawyers or tax advisers or auditors during a tax, program, or financial audit. Preparing your own meeting summary forms in advance may save you time and money later.

FORMS ON CD-ROM

Below is a sample of the Meeting Summary Sheet included on the CD-ROM at the back of the book. (A copy of the form is also in Appendix C.) Fill it out following the special instructions provided.

Meeting Summary Sheet

Name of Nonprofit: _____

Year: _____

Type of Meeting: ☐ Annual/Regular ☐ Special **1**

Meeting of: ☐ Directors ☐ Members

☐ _____ Committee **1**

Date: _____ Time: _____ **2** _____

Place: _____ **3** _____

Meeting Called By: _____ **4** _____

Purpose: _____ **5** _____

Committee or Other Reports or Presentations: _____ **6** _____

_____

Other Reminders or Notes: _____

_____

_____

Notice Required: ☐ Written ☐ Verbal ☐ Not Required **7**

Notice Must Be Given by Date: _____ **8** _____

Notice of Meeting Given To: **9**

Name	Type of Notice*	Location or Phone Number	Date Notice Given	Date Acknowledged Receipt

* Types of Notice: written (mailed, hand-delivered), verbal (in-person, telephone conversation, answering machine, voice mail), email, fax.

Special Instructions

1 Check the type of meeting, whether it is annual (sometimes called a regular meeting in the bylaws) or special. Indicate whether it is a directors', committee, or members' meeting.

2 If you know the meeting date and time, fill that in. If you expect to hold a special meeting but are not sure of the exact date, make a note anyway of the possible meeting date as a reminder.

3 Show the location of the meeting. The most likely location for meetings is the nonprofit's principal office.

4 Special meetings of the board, committees, or members are called by those authorized to do so under the bylaws. Special meetings usually may be called by directors, the president, a committee chair, a specified percentage of the members of the corporation, or others authorized in the bylaws or under state law. (See Step 3, below, for more on calling meetings.)

Meetings Held in Cyberspace

You may decide to hold your meeting via a conference telephone call, a video conference (webcam) hookup, or even a virtual meeting via a conference on a local intranet or Internet site. If you use any of these technology-enabled meeting methods, make sure to specify the location and method of holding the meeting on the Meeting Summary Sheet—for example, "a webcam/audio Internet conference among the following individuals at the following locations: (*names and physical or Internet addresses of attendees*)."

5 For all upcoming meetings, set forth a brief statement of the purpose. The purpose of an annual members' meeting will usually include "the election of directors of the corporation."

The purpose of annual directors' meetings is normally: "acceptance by directors of their election to the board for another term, discussion of the past year's operations and results, planning of the upcoming year's operations and goals, and the transaction of any other proper business that may be brought before the meeting." If additional items of business are on the agenda, state them separately as well.

6 Indicate any committee, staff, adviser (lawyer, accountant, other expert), or other reports or recommendations that will be presented at the meeting.

7 Check the type of notice required for the meeting, whether written or verbal, and the date by which the required notice must be mailed or given to the directors, committee participants, or members. If no notice is required—if, for example, your bylaws dispense with the requirement for notice of an upcoming directors' meeting—check the "Not Required" box.

Make sure you provide at least the required notice for meetings as specified in your bylaws. As a matter of courtesy and common sense, many nonprofits give their members and directors at least three or four weeks' advance notice of all annual meetings, and as much notice as possible of special meetings. (See Step 5, below, for a discussion of notice requirements.)

8 Enter the date by which you need to send out or personally provide notice to the meeting participants.

9 Once notice is actually given, fill in this portion of the form to show who received notice prior to the meeting.

For each person given notice, show the date and manner in which notice was given for a meeting and whether the person acknowledged receiving notice. If you prepared or received any other documentation regarding the notice (see the Acknowledgment of Receipt and Certification of Mailing forms in Step 9 and at the end of this chapter), make a note that this material has been placed in the meeting folder or corporate records.

TIP

Laws or not, everyone appreciates formal notice of meetings.
We suggest you provide prior written notice of all directors' and members'
meetings stating the time, place, and purpose of the meeting, even if your
bylaws or state law don't require it. Telephone and email can work but aren't
as effective as mailed notification, and don't provide a paper trail. If you're
going to go to the trouble of holding a meeting, why not make extra sure
that everyone knows where and when it will be, and why you're holding it?
Our advice goes double if you plan to consider and vote on any issues about
which there may be disagreement. If dissenting members or directors believe
you are trying to take action at a "secret meeting," you're practically inviting
controversy and dissension.

Step 3. Call the Meeting

The first step toward holding a special meeting of directors,
members, or a committee, is to "call" the meeting. This doesn't
mean getting on the phone to a bunch of people and saying "Let's
meet tomorrow, 5:00." It has a narrower legal meaning—essentially
that someone makes an internal request within the organization
that a meeting be scheduled (after which actual notifications can
go out). Only special meetings need to be called—no one needs
to formally call an annual or regular meeting because they're
prescheduled, as discussed under "Preparing for Annual and
Regular Meetings," below.

Under state law or your bylaws, only certain people have the
power to call meetings. Typically, bylaws allow the president (or
chair of the board), members of the board, a specified percentage
of members, a committee chair, or others to call a special meeting.
After the special meeting is called, the secretary provides notice of
the meeting to all persons entitled to attend.

Check your bylaws to determine who may call special meetings of your nonprofit. If you have any questions, check your state's Nonprofit Corporation Act.

Preparing for Annual and Regular Meetings

Regular or annual meetings of directors or members are already scheduled in the bylaws, so no one needs to take the first step of calling the meeting. Still, someone needs to remind everyone about these meetings so that the premeeting work gets done. The secretary or chair is usually the person designated to stay on top of annual and regular meetings. Whoever is in charge, the Meeting Summary Sheet discussed in Step 2, above, can help serve as a reminder of this task.

Who May Call Special Meetings

Special meetings must be called by someone who is legally authorized to do so. Here are the typical rules:

- **Special meetings of directors.** Standard bylaws and state law typically require that special meetings of the board of directors be called by the president or other chief presiding officer, the director who acts as chairperson of the board, or a specified number of directors. Other officers may be allowed to call special board meetings as well; check your bylaws.
- **Special meetings of members.** Special meetings of members must ordinarily be called by a majority vote of the board of directors, by a certain percentage of the members of the corporation, by the president of the corporation, or by persons authorized to do so in the bylaws. Again, check your bylaws.

- **Committee meetings.** Almost all committee meetings are special meetings because they usually are not scheduled in the bylaws. For committees of the board (composed of at least two or more directors who can transact board business), the rules for calling special directors' meeting normally apply. However, for other types of committees, which we call "advisory" committees, state law usually lets the nonprofit decide who may call the meetings. Typically, nonprofit bylaws allow the board of directors, committee chair, or a specified number of committee members to call an advisory committee meeting.

How to Call a Meeting

If you're one of the select few in your organization who is authorized to call for a meeting to be held, how do you go about it? Neither your state laws nor your bylaws may say a word about this (but check your bylaws just to be sure). If you don't encounter any legal guidelines, you're free to either speak to or write a letter or email to any corporate director or officer. To be on the safe side, however, we suggest calls of all important meetings be made by written request to the corporate secretary. However made, the call should allow enough time to:

- provide members or directors with ample notice of the meeting (see Step 5, below), and
- prepare any necessary materials, presentations, or motions for the meeting.

At times, smaller nonprofits—where directors and members are in close contact and on good terms—can do fine calling a meeting orally. However, larger organizations or those planning to convene a membership meeting to discuss an important item should always make a written call of the meeting to create a record of the fact that the meeting was properly called.

EXAMPLE: Think Green, Inc., a grassroots environmental education nonprofit, starts out with a small board and just a few volunteer members. During the early years, special meetings are called by someone telephoning each director and member. As the group grows, requests for special meetings are made in writing to the secretary, who prepares formal written notices that are delivered to each person entitled to attend the meeting.

Prepare a Call of Meeting Form

It's handy to use a written Call of Meeting form for sending requests to the corporate secretary. This form should specify the date, time, and place of the meeting, as well as its purpose.

FORMS ON CD-ROM

Below is a sample of the Call of Meeting form. Fill it out following the special instructions provided below. (A copy of the form is also in Appendix C.)

Call of Meeting

To:

Secretary: _____

Name of nonprofit: _____

Address of nonprofit: _____

_____

The following person(s): **1**

Name	Title
_____	_____
_____	_____

authorized under provisions of the bylaws of __[name of nonprofit corporation]__ ,
hereby make(s) a call and request to hold a(n) __[special, annual, or regular]__ **2**
meeting of the __[directors or members]__ of the corporation for the purpose(s) of:
3 _____ .

The date and time of the meeting requested is: **4** _____ .

The requested location for the meeting is: [the principal office of the corporation
or other location] **5** , state of _____ .

The secretary is requested to provide all proper notices as required by the bylaws
of the corporation and any other necessary materials to all persons entitled to
attend the meeting.

Date: **6** _____

Signed: **6** _____

Special Instructions

1 List the name of each person calling the meeting. In the column to the right of the name, show whether the person is a director, officer, committee member, or member of the corporation.

2 Fill in "special," "annual," or "regular." Annual or regular meetings normally do not have to be called; they're already scheduled in the corporate bylaws. However, if you want to call the meeting as a way of keeping track of the meeting date, it's fine to do so.

3 In the blanks after the words "for the purpose(s) of," briefly state the purpose of the meeting. Here are some suggestions.

Annual meeting of members: "Electing the directors of the corporation."

Annual (or regular) meeting of directors: "Review of the prior year's operations, discussion of corporate operations for the upcoming year, acceptance by the directors of another term of office on the board, and transaction of any other business that may properly come before the meeting."

Special meetings: state the specific purpose for which the meeting was called, for example, "Discussion of upcoming fundraising program."

4 If appropriate, state the specific date or general time frame in which you wish the meeting to be held, such as "January 15, 2010, at 10:00 a.m.," "first Monday in June," or "latter half of the month of October." If an annual meeting, specify the time and date scheduled for the meeting in the bylaws.

5 State the location of the meeting.

6 Date the form and have each person making the call sign below the date.

When you've completed the form, place it in the folder for the upcoming meeting or in the corporate records book.

Step 4. Your Meeting Participant List

Everyone who is legally entitled to be notified of an upcoming meeting will need to receive notice. By preparing a Meeting Participant List, you'll organize your records and make sure that no one is overlooked.

If you're preparing for a members' meeting, your state may require you to prepare a members list within a few days of the date notice is first sent out and that you make it available before and during the meeting for inspection by other members (check your bylaws). If the list isn't available for inspection, you risk a complaining member petitioning a court to have the meeting postponed. This sort of squabbling usually occurs only in large nonprofits where members need to contact and petition other members or assess the strength of another membership faction prior to a members' meeting.

The list should be in alphabetical order, showing the name and address of each meeting participant, and, if a member, the voting power of the member (normally one vote per member). If your organization has issued different classes or series of voting memberships, the names should be listed alphabetically within separate membership voting groups. As always, remember that we are referring to voting power held by those who hold formal voting memberships in your nonprofit. If your meeting participants include only honorary, advisory, or contributing members who do not have voting power, you can simply list their names and addresses on your meeting participant list, along with their title ("advisory member" or some other title).

Sensible Reasons to Keep Lists of Meeting Participants

Whether or not you're required to prepare a member list, it makes sense for your secretary to keep an up-to-date list of your organization's directors, officers, members, and committee members and participants for all meetings. By doing this, you'll keep track of everyone entitled to receive notice of and attend all meetings, while complying with any members' list requirements in your state.

One easy way to meet the membership list requirement is to use your membership roster (see Chapter 1) or keep a member ledger in your corporate records book, listing the names and addresses of your members. Then, simply bring your corporate records book with this information to all members' meetings

FORMS ON CD-ROM

Below is a sample of the Meeting Participant List included on the CD-ROM. Fill it out following the special instructions provided below. (A copy of the form is also in Appendix C.)

Meeting Participant List

Name of Nonprofit: _____

Type of Meeting: ☐ Annual/Regular ☐ Special **(1)**

Meeting of: ☐ Directors ☐ Members

☐ _____ Committee **(2)**

Date: **(3)** _____

Meeting Participants (list names in alphabetical order): **(4)**

Name: _____

Address: _____

Telephone: _____

☐ Director

☐ Member: Type of Membership and Number of Votes: _____

☐ Committee Member

☐ Officer: Title _____

☐ Other (position and reason for attendance): _____

_____

Name: _____

Address: _____

Telephone: _____

☐ Director

☐ Member: Type of Membership and Number of Votes: _____

☐ Committee Member

☐ Officer: Title _____

☐ Other (position and reason for attendance): _____

_____

Special Instructions

1 Specify what type of meeting you are holding.

2 State whether it's a meeting of your directors, members, or a committee.

3 Fill in the meeting date.

4 Fill in (in alphabetical order) the names, addresses, and phone numbers of:

- all directors, members, or committee members entitled to attend the upcoming meeting, and
- others who may attend the meeting, including officers who will present reports at the meeting.

   If you need to fill in more names than the form allows, copy the paragraphs providing information about meeting participants as many times as needed.

   For members' meetings, you will normally list all current members of the nonprofit, unless:

- some nonvoting memberships have been issued to members, or
- the board has set a record date for the meeting that restricts the number of members who can vote at the meeting. (The record date is the date by which a member must have become a member to be able to vote at the meeting.)

When you've completed the form, place it in the folder for the upcoming meeting or in the corporate records book.

New Members' Rights Regarding Meetings

If someone becomes a member of your organization today, is that person entitled to receive notice of tomorrow's meeting, and attend and vote? Not necessarily. Nonprofit membership bylaws may set a date by which a member must have become a member in order to be entitled to receive notice of and vote at an upcoming members' meeting. This date is called a record date.

If the bylaws do not set a record date, the board of directors may do so. State law may limit how far in advance a record date may be set—for example, no more than 60 or 70 days prior to the meeting. If no record date is set by the bylaws or directors, state law may set a default record date for the meeting, typically the day prior to the date the notice of the meeting is mailed or given to a member or, if no notice is given, the day prior to the meeting date. To be safe (and fair), you should provide notice to all members listed on the corporate records on the day preceding the day the first notice is mailed or personally given to a member.

Step 5. Give Notice of the Meeting

Your next step is to provide directors, committee participants, or members with notice of the time, place, and purpose of the meeting. If your bylaws do not specify how to do this, we suggest commonsense compliance procedures for providing notice of all meetings. These should satisfy even the most stringent state law requirements.

Always Give Notice (Even If It's Not Required)

First, an important practical point: Even when notice of a meeting is not legally required (as is likely the case for the annual directors' and members' meetings scheduled in your bylaws), you should always provide it, unless you have all directors or all members sign a waiver of notice form. Your directors and members can't be expected to remember or dig these dates out of your corporate bylaws. As a matter of courtesy—and so that you're not sitting at an empty table—they should always be informed well in advance of the time, place, and purpose of all meetings.

That advice is doubly important if board members or key members are likely to disagree on important decisions. The last thing you want is to hold a meeting, go through intense discussions until you arrive at a big decision, then have a director or member come back and try to set it aside based on a claim that a meeting was not properly noticed.

To exceed any state's legal notice requirements, simply follow these rules:

Rule 1. Provide *written* notice of all meetings.

Rule 2. Provide notice at least ten business days (two full weeks) prior to directors' and committee meetings—unless your bylaws require a longer notice period.

Rule 3. Provide notice at least 20 business days (four full weeks) prior to members' meetings (unless your bylaws require a longer notice period).

Rule 4. State the purpose of the meeting in the notice.

If you follow these suggestions, you should be in compliance with even the strictest statutory notice of meeting rules.

If a Meeting Can't Be Finished in One Day

If a meeting runs so long that you have to stop and carry it over to another time in order to conclude the unfinished business, the second meeting is referred to as an adjourned meeting. (Don't be confused by the fact that finishing a meeting is also referred to as adjourning the meeting.)

If a members' meeting is continued to another time, it's possible you won't be required to send out notice of the continued (adjourned) meeting unless a new record date is set (establishing new memberships) or the meeting is scheduled for a much later date. For example, state law may require a new notice if the adjourned meeting will be held more than 45 days after the date of the first meeting.

If a directors' meeting is adjourned, you'll most likely have to give notice of the new meeting to any directors who weren't at the original meeting. Check your bylaws or state law.

We recommend you send out new notice for any adjourned meeting, whether a directors', committee, or members' meeting. Memories are short and schedules crowded with other commitments. Besides, providing a new notice gives any members or directors who happened to miss the first meeting a chance to attend the second (as state law may require).

State Law Notice Requirements

Let's look at state requirements for providing notice of directors' and members' meetings. (We won't go into advisory committee meetings, about which state law is often silent.) Remember: Laws change and exceptions may exist. Check your bylaws, and if your bylaws do not specify a rule, check your state law to find your state's specific rules.

Directors' Meetings

State notice requirements for directors' meetings are somewhat lenient, because directors are already expected to participate in your organization's affairs on a regular basis.

Annual or regular directors' meetings. The laws of many states allow the nonprofit to set its own notice requirements for directors' annual and regular meetings in the bylaws. In states without specified rules, it is common for bylaws to dispense with notice requirements for annual or regular meetings of the board.

Special directors' meetings. For special meetings, many states require that notice be given to directors. The required notice period is usually anywhere from two to four days prior to the meeting, unless the bylaws specify a longer or shorter notice period. In addition, a shorter notice period may be allowed for personal notice, such as telephone notice.

Manner of giving notice to directors. Generally, state law allows notice to directors to be given orally or in writing. It must include the date, time, and place of the meeting. Most state laws don't require that the purpose of the directors' meeting be placed in the notice; however, it's a good idea to do so—particularly for special meetings.

Members' Meetings

The state law rules for providing notice of members' meetings are stricter than those for directors' meetings.

Regular and special meetings. In all states, written notice of the date, place, and time of all members' meetings, whether annual or special, must be given to members. Typically, notice must be given no more than 90 (sometimes no more than 60 or 50) and not fewer than ten (sometimes fewer, such as five) days before the meeting.

Members legally entitled to notice. All members who will have voting power at the meeting are entitled, in most states, to receive written notice of the meeting.

CAUTION

Manner of giving notice to members. All member notices should be in writing. The notice should state the time, place, and date of the upcoming meeting. The purpose of the meeting should also be placed in all notices (even though some states may allow standard items of business to be approved at annual members' meetings even if not stated in the notice). For special members' meetings, state law usually provides that only the matters listed in the notice for the meeting can be approved by the members at the meeting.

Prepare a Notice of Meeting Form

If you have decided to provide written notice of an upcoming meeting, fill in the Notice of Meeting form included on the enclosed CD-ROM as you follow the sample form and instructions.

FORMS ON CD-ROM

Below is a sample of the Notice of Meeting form included on the CD-ROM. Fill it out following the special instructions provided below. (A copy of the form is also in Appendix C.)

Notice of Meeting
of
[Name of Nonprofit]

A(n) _[annual, regular, or special]_ **(1)** meeting of the _[directors or members or committee]_ **(2)** of _[name of nonprofit]_ will be held at _[location of meeting]_ **(3)**, state of _____, on _____**(4)**_____, 20_____ at _____ : _____ ___ m.

The purpose(s) of the meeting is/are as follows: **(5)** _____
_____
_____ .

(6) [_Optional—For membership proxy organizations only._] If you are a member and cannot attend the meeting and wish to designate another person to vote your membership for you, please deliver a signed membership proxy form to the secretary of the corporation before the meeting. Contact the secretary if you need help obtaining or preparing this form.

Signature of Secretary: _____

Name of Secretary: _____

Nonprofit corporation: _____

Address: _____
_____ .

Phone: _____ Fax: _____

Special Instructions

1 If the meeting is scheduled in your bylaws, use the term annual or regular. (Some bylaws schedule more than one meeting per year for directors or members; if so, these are normally called regular meetings instead of annual meetings.) For all other meetings, insert special.

2 State whether it's a meeting for directors, members, or a committee.

3 Meetings are normally held at the principal office of the corporation, although state law and bylaws usually allow directors', committee, and members' meetings to be held anywhere within or outside the state.

4 Make sure you schedule the meeting far enough in advance to comply with state law and bylaw requirements. If you don't have time to give the required notice, then make sure to have each director, committee participant, or member sign a written waiver of notice form (see below). You can still prepare and send out a Notice of Meeting form as explained here to give advance notice to your directors, committee participants, or members, but it will not be legally effective.

5 Succinctly state the purpose(s) of the meeting. Here are some suggestions:

- **Annual meeting of members:** "electing the directors of the corporation"
- **Annual (or regular) meeting of directors:** "reviewing the prior year's operations, discussing operations for the upcoming year, acceptance by the directors of another term of office on the board, and transaction of any other business that may properly come before the meeting," or
- **Special meetings:** state the specific purpose for which the meeting was called, for example, "approval of grant from _____ Foundation."

CROSS-REFERENCE

Sending background material. As discussed in Step 8, below, you will probably want to send out additional background material with your notice to help your directors, committee participants, or members understand the issues to be discussed at the upcoming meeting.

CAUTION

Make sure to state the purposes of special members' meetings in the written notice form. Under most bylaws, you can't approve any items at a special members' meeting unless the general nature of the proposal was included in a written notice (or waiver of notice) of the meeting. If you follow our suggestions above, you've already met this requirement.

TIP

Use an agenda to give notice of all items to be considered at a meeting. One way to fully inform all potential participants of the business to be proposed at the meeting is to prepare and send out an agenda for the meeting, listing all of the items and business that will be discussed or proposed for approval. We discuss the preparation of an agenda in Step 6, below. If you decide to do this, fill in this blank as follows: "see the enclosed agenda for the meeting."

6 This is an optional paragraph that you may wish to include in a notice for an upcoming members' meeting if membership proxies are authorized in your bylaws. It alerts members of their legal right to notify the secretary of the corporation prior to the meeting if they wish to have another person vote for them at the meeting (make sure your bylaws allow this). (For instructions on preparing a proxy form for an upcoming members' meeting, see Step 10, below.)

Waivers of Notice

In some circumstances, you might want or need to forgo notice of a meeting for your board or members. For example, you may simply not have time to provide notice. The solution is to use a waiver of notice of meeting form. Most state corporate laws allow waiver of notice for directors' and members' meetings.

Waivers for directors' meetings. Most states allow directors to sign a written waiver of notice of meeting. Typically, state laws also provide that even if a director didn't get proper formal notice of a meeting, but hears about it and attends, by the act of showing up the director legally waives notice to the meeting—unless he or she speaks up at the beginning and objects to not having received proper notice.

Waivers for members' meetings. Most states allow members to sign a written waiver of notice of meeting form, and, as with directors, provide that members who attend a meeting without objection are assumed to have agreed to the notice or lack of notice for the meeting.

Check your bylaws to determine the waiver of notice rules that apply to your nonprofit.

 TIP

Always clearly state the purpose of the meeting in the waiver. In some cases, it is legally required. In any case, it will help make sure all directors and members know the nature of the business to be taken up at the meeting. (State laws often prohibit the transaction of any business not specified in the notice or waiver of notice for a special members' meeting.)

You can prepare one Waiver of Notice of Meeting form for multiple directors or members to sign, or you can prepare one form for each person.

Waiver of Notice of Meeting

of

[name of nonprofit]

The undersigned _[names of directors or members]_ hereby waive notice of and consent to the holding of the _[annual, special, or regular]_ meeting of the _[directors or members]_ of _[name of corporation]_ held at _[location of meeting]_ , state of _____, on (**1**) _____ , 20 _____ at _____ : _____ ___ m. for the purposes of: _____

_____ .

Dated: (**2**) _____

Signature _____   Printed Name _____

_____   _____

_____   _____

_____   _____

_____   _____

_____   _____

_____   _____

FORMS ON CD-ROM

The sample of the Waiver of Notice of Meeting form, above, is included on the CD-ROM. Fill it out following the special instructions below.

Special Instructions

1 Under state corporate statutes, for certain important corporate decisions such as the election of directors or amendment of bylaws, a waiver of notice form must contain a description of the matter presented and approved at a meeting. When preparing a waiver of notice form, we recommend you always state the purpose of the meeting. Be as specific as you can regarding the proposals to be presented at the meeting.

2 If more than one person will sign the form, the date inserted here should be the date the first person signs the waiver form. This date should be on or before the meeting date.

Step 6. Prepare an Agenda

A written agenda that lists the order of business for the meeting helps give a sense of purpose and direction to the meeting. The agenda provides a framework for the meeting and keeps the discussion on track. An agenda also can help the chairperson keep an eye on the clock, making sure that all proposed items are covered within the total time allotted.

All agendas should include:
- meeting start time
- meeting end time
- meeting location
- items of business to be discussed
- time allotted for each item of business, and
- the name of the person in charge of each item of business.

The agenda should be sent out to all meeting participants with any other premeeting information that is ready ahead of time.

Step 7. Prepare Drafts of Resolutions

Sometimes it makes sense to prepare a draft of any resolutions or motions that you plan to introduce at the meeting ahead of time— particularly if it relates to something complicated or controversial, or if you want to give your directors or members time to consider the issue. This might be useful, for example, if you wanted to amend your articles or bylaws and you know ahead of time the exact language you would like to get approved.

You don't need to use fancy or legal language for your resolution; just describe as specifically as you can the transaction or matter to be approved by your board or members in a short, concise statement. Here are some examples:

EXAMPLE 1: (BANK LOAN) "The board resolved that the treasurer be authorized to obtain a loan from [*name of bank*] for the amount of $_____ on commercially reasonable terms."

EXAMPLE 2: (HIRING): "The board approved the hiring of [*name of new employee*], hired in the position of [*job title*] at an annual salary of $_____ and in accordance with the terms of the corporation's standard employment contract."

EXAMPLE 3: (TAX YEAR) "The board decided that the corporation shall adopt a tax year with an ending date of December 31."

EXAMPLE 4: (AMENDMENT OF BYLAWS) "The members resolved that the following new section be added to the corporation's bylaws: [*title and language of new section*]."

Step 8. Assemble a Premeeting Information Packet

To prepare people adequately for a meeting, especially those who are not involved in the day-to-day management of the organization, you should provide them with as much of the meeting material as you can ahead of time. You can include the meeting materials when you send out your notice of an upcoming meeting to directors, committee participants, or members. You may want to provide this material even if you do not send out a formal written notice of the meeting. (For example, if you provide verbal notice of an annual members' meeting or dispense with notice completely by having members or directors sign a written consent.)

Instead of mailing hard copies of meeting materials, some groups post their meeting materials on the Internet or send them by email. If you decide to provide your materials electronically, make sure everyone is capable of receiving the documents that way or offer to send hard copies to anyone who prefers hard copies.

Your premeeting information packet should include:

- **An agenda for the meeting.** This should list new business, as well as any unfinished business from a prior meeting.
- **Copies of reports, presentations, and background material.** Include all materials that may help your directors, committee participants, or members become informed on the issues to be decided upon. Doing this not only saves time at the meeting, but helps your nonprofit make better decisions.
- **Copies of any proposed motions or resolutions that will be voted on.**
- **Minutes of the last members', committee, or directors' meeting.** If you want to approve the minutes from the last meeting, include a copy. To save time at the meeting, you may wish to enclose an approval form with your prior minutes to allow directors, committee participants, or members to sign off on the last meeting's minutes before the upcoming meeting.

- **Member proxies.** You may include a blank proxy form with notice of a members' meeting if you allow membership voting by proxy in your bylaws. (See Step 10, below.)
- **Proof of receipt.** If you want the members, committee participants, or directors to acknowledge that they received notice of the meeting, send an Acknowledgment of Receipt of Notice of Meeting form to be signed and returned. (See Step 9, below.)

Step 9. Acknowledgment of Receipt Forms

For important or controversial meetings, you may wish to dot all the "i"s and cross all the "t"s by preparing documentation that shows all directors, committee participants, or members actually received notice of the meeting. This may be particularly important if you have outside directors or members and don't follow our advice to provide written notice to everyone (for example, you call or provide some kind of oral notice instead). Below are procedures and forms you can use to create a record that notice was properly received by your directors or members.

FORMS ON CD-ROM

Below is a sample of the Acknowledgement of Receipt of Notice of Meeting form included on the CD-ROM. Note that you should fill out a separate form for each person who acknowledges notice.

Acknowledgment of Receipt of Notice of Meeting

I received notice of a(n) *[annual, regular, or special]* meeting of the *[directors or members]* of *[name of corporation]* on *[leave date blank]* , _____ . The notice of meeting stated the date, time, place, and purpose of the upcoming meeting.

The notice of meeting was: (**1**)

☐ received by fax

☐ delivered orally to me in person

☐ delivered orally to me by phone call

☐ left in a message on an answering machine or voice mail

☐ delivered by mail

☐ delivered via email

☐ other: _____

Dated: _____ (**2**) _____

Signed: _____

Printed Name: _____

Please return to: (**3**)

Name: _____

Nonprofit corporation: _____

Address: _____

Phone: _____ Fax: _____

Special Instructions

1 Check the box to indicate how notice was received.

2 The person who received the notice should date and sign the form. You may print his or her name on the appropriate line.

3 To ensure that you receive the acknowledgment, fill in the secretary's name, address (include city, state, and zip), and fax number.

Place a copy of the acknowledgment in the folder for the upcoming meeting or in your corporate records book.

Step 10. Proxies for Members' Meetings

A written proxy lets a member authorize another person to vote his or her shares at an upcoming members' meeting. Your bylaws may authorize the use of written membership proxies. Larger nonprofits, or those with members scattered across a wide geographic region, may routinely include a blank proxy form with the notice and other premeeting materials sent to members. For smaller groups, there is no legal requirement or practical necessity to routinely send out proxy forms. This is because most of the time there is no conflict among members and no desire on the part of a member who will miss a meeting to authorize someone else to vote in his or her place. However, in rare instances, you may be asked to provide a proxy to a member prior to an upcoming meeting.

 FORMS ON CD-ROM

Below is a sample of the Proxy form included on the CD-ROM. (A copy of the form is also in Appendix C.) Fill it out following the special instructions provided below.

Proxy

The undersigned member of __[name of nonprofit corporation]__ authorizes

① _____ to act as his/her proxy and

to represent and vote his/her membership at a(n) __[regular, annual, or special]__

meeting of members to be held at __[location of meeting]__ , state of _____ ,

on _____② _____ , _____ at _____ : _____ __ m.

Dated: _____

Signed: _____

Printed Name: _____

Please return proxy by _____③ _____ , _____ **to:**

Name: _____④ _____

Title: _____

Nonprofit corporation: _____

Address: _____

City, State, Zip: _____

Phone: _____ Fax: _____

Special Instructions

1 Leave a blank line here. The member will insert the name of the proxyholder—this is the person who is authorized by the member to vote his or her membership at the upcoming meeting of members.

2 Some statutes and bylaws limit the validity of a written proxy to a six-month period (though a typical time limit is 11 months if no limit is stated in the proxy; the maximum stated limit normally allowed for a proxy is three years).

3 Insert the date by which the proxy must be returned to the corporate secretary. This date is usually before the meeting so the secretary knows in advance that a proxyholder will be attending the meeting.

4 Normally, proxies are sent out by and returned to the corporate secretary.

Remember to place copies of all completed proxies in the folder or corporate records book for the members' meeting to which they apply.

Step 11. How to Deliver Notice and the Information Packet

Have the secretary of your organization mail or personally deliver the Notice of Meeting form to whomever should receive it, together with any premeeting information you prepared under Step 8, above. If the information is mailed, use the exact address of the director, committee participant, or member as shown in your corporate records. On the Meeting Summary Sheet, (Step 2, above), have the secretary complete the lines at the bottom of the form indicating how and when each director, committee participant, or member was given the notice form. Place the notated Meeting Summary Sheet in your master folder for the meeting or your corporate records book.

When to Use Certified Mail

Using first class mail for mailed notices of meetings is all that's usually legally required. However, if you have dissident directors or members, or have some other reason that you want to be able to show that a person actually received mailed notice, send these materials by certified mail with a return receipt requested (or by express mail with signature tracking). Place the certification number or return receipt in your meeting folder or corporate records book.

Other Ways to Provide Notice

You may occasionally decide to provide notice of corporate meetings orally, in person, or by phone, answering machine, voicemail, or email. This is particularly likely to happen in small, newly formed nonprofits where a few people actively manage and operate the organization. If you give notice orally or by email, you should still prepare documentation showing how and when the notice was given.

There are a number of electronic ways to provide and prove the giving of notice to directors and members. For example, you may decide to fax or email notice of an upcoming meeting instead of personally delivering or mailing written notice. Although not specifically authorized under many corporate statutes, faxing or using email to send a written notice to a director, committee participant, or member should meet the substance, if not letter, of legal notice requirements. Of course, the notice must be received by the director, committee participant, or member within the proper number of days before the meeting.

Whatever method you use, be sure to take sensible steps to show that notice was properly sent to or received by your directors, committee participants, or members within the proper number of days before the meeting. (In Step 9, above, we explain methods of proving receipt of notice of meeting by directors, committee participants, and members.)

In-House Certification of Mailing Form

If you don't want to take the time to send notices by certified mail, you can prepare an in-house certification of mailing form. In this form, your corporate secretary certifies that notice for an upcoming meeting was properly mailed to directors, committee participants, or members. Include the date notice was mailed and how it was sent.

Make sure to attach a copy of the notice to the mailing form, and place this paperwork in your meeting folder or corporate records book. ●

The Big Day—Holding Your Meeting

N ow it's time to hold your meeting. You've done all the pre-meeting notice and preparation work for your meeting. Now we'll go over what you can to do to make your actual meeting successful and productive.

As always, one of the first questions we ask is whether state law imposes any relevant rules. The answer is that most state laws don't, aside from quorum and voting requirements (which we'll also cover in this chapter). For the most part, it'll be up to you to decide how you want to conduct your meeting and how each person does his or her job.

Decide What Rules You'll Follow

Many people's first instinct is to avoid using formal meetings rules, fearing they'll be restrictive and make everyone sound like stuffy parliamentarians. Indeed, for a small group, where all the directors are actively engaged in the organization, you might be able to go without formal procedures. However, most nonprofits benefit from having a formal set of rules for their meetings, including how a proposal or resolution is raised, discussed, submitted for a vote, and voted on. It's best to design and adopt procedural rules that fit your style and the size of your group.

The most widely used meeting rules are *Robert's Rules of Order*. The book is available at bookstores and online at www.robertsrules. com. Or, you can follow formal parliamentary procedures. For a remarkably easy-to-use guide to the most commonly used parliamentary procedures at meetings, see *Parliamentary Law at a Glance*, by E.C. Utter (The Reilly & Lee Co.).

Gather at Your Meeting Location

The first step is for your directors, members, or committee members to meet at the time and place specified in your notice of the meeting. As long as they've gotten proper notice, they'll hopefully show up, prepared and ready to go. Of course, there will be times when someone will either forget or need to cancel due to last minute emergencies or major conflicts. If that's the case, always let your chair or president know ahead of time if possible so he or she can figure out whether this will create a quorum problem.

Appoint a Chairperson and Secretary

The chairperson and secretary play important roles at meetings. Usually whoever has been appointed to the board officer position of president (or chair) acts as chair at meetings and the board secretary takes on the role of secretary at meetings. If, for any reason, your chair or secretary is not available for a meeting, you'll need to appoint someone to take on those responsibilities at the meeting.

The Role of the Meeting Chairperson

The chair is responsible for presiding over meetings and making sure they proceed in an orderly and efficient manner. The chair often goes item by item through the agenda trying to stay within the allotted time, and then asks for votes on anything that requires action.

The Role of the Secretary

Someone different from the chairperson must act as secretary of the meeting. He or she is responsible for taking notes on each item of business covered and recording the outcome of anything discussed and voted upon. In the minutes forms presented in later chapters, we assume that you follow the common practice of having your board secretary act as secretary for the meeting.

Your secretary does not need to provide a longhand narrative of all the happenings at a meeting. It is usually enough to list who is present, the nature of the proposals raised, and the outcome of votes taken. This is the information the secretary will need to prepare the final minutes of the meeting.

The secretary can prepare the minutes at the meeting using a computer and the minutes form on the CD-ROM. Or, he or she can take notes and then prepare the minutes later. Normally you submit the minutes for approval at the next meeting of your directors, committee, or members. After they are approved, the secretary signs them and then places them in the corporate records book.

Call the Meeting to Order

The chairperson usually calls the meeting to order by announcing that it's time to begin. The chair then directs the order in which business will be covered. That usually involves introducing each item of business on the agenda and then either leading the discussion or calling on someone else to take the lead. For example, the chairperson may ask the secretary to read a proposal or members of the finance committee to present a report.

Make Sure That a Quorum Is Present

If you don't have enough people present, you can't hold a meeting, much less approve any business. The secretary should note who is present and absent, then make sure that the minimum number—a so-called "quorum" of directors or members—is in attendance. "Present" doesn't necessarily mean physically present at the meeting location. Most states allow people to participate by conference call or other electronic means as long as everyone can hear each other simultaneously. (See "Holding a Meeting in Cyberspace" in Chapter 2). If you come up short of a quorum, the chairperson should adjourn the meeting to a new time and date.

Your bylaws will probably tell you the quorum requirements for directors' and members' meetings. Below we discuss the quorum requirements that most nonprofits have in their bylaws. If you are having a meeting of a "committee of the board"—that is, a committee with two or more directors that has the authority to act in place of the board—then you'll probably need to follow the same rules. We don't discuss advisory committee requirements because generally a nonprofit is free to adopt whatever rules it wants for advisory committees. (See "Board Committees and Advisory Committees May Not Follow the Same Rules" in "Chapter 3.)

Quorum Rules for Directors' Meetings

Oftentimes, the quorum for directors' meetings is set at a majority of the authorized number of directors. The authorized number of directors is the total number of slots on your board, whether or not each board position is filled. Some states allow nonprofit corporations to set a higher or lower than majority quorum in their bylaws, as long as any lesser quorum requirement does not fall below a set statutory minimum (often established as one-third of the full board). For example, smaller nonprofits—those with five or fewer members—may wish to ensure a significant director presence by imposing a two-thirds quorum requirement for board meetings. Conversely, nonprofits with larger boards may feel encumbered with a majority-quorum rule and may decide to set a board quorum at a less-than-majority percentage or number—for example, one-third of the directors or eight out of 20 directors.

> **EXAMPLE:** The bylaws of Eco-Vision, an environmental non-profit, state that the corporation must have seven directors and that a majority of the authorized number of directors represents a quorum for directors' meetings. At their spring meeting, only three people show up, because one board slot is vacant, two directors have conflicts, and one simply forgets. Unfortunately, the organization needs four directors to attend board meetings to reach a quorum, even if a slot on the board is vacant. That means they can't approve any business at the meeting.

> **CAUTION**
>
> **No quorum?** It's fine to chat for a bit, until you're sure that the absent members won't be showing up, but don't take any substantive action. Simply adjourn the meeting until another time when a quorum of directors can be present.

Quorum Rules for Members' Meetings

A quorum for members' meetings is usually set by bylaws (and state law) as a majority of the membership votes entitled to vote on an issue. Unlike the director-meeting quorum rule, this rule relates to the number of votes, not the number of people present at a meeting. However, because the default state law rule (which most nonprofits follow) is that each member gets one vote, the typical quorum requirement for most membership nonprofits is that a majority of members must be present (in person or by proxy) to hold a members' meeting.

What if your articles or bylaws say something different? Some states permit you to follow your own rule. In some states, the membership quorum can be set as low as 10% of the full voting membership of the nonprofit, except for certain major actions such as amending the articles or bylaws. Further, some states allow a less-than-majority membership quorum for a meeting as long as the members vote only on items that are in the notice for the meeting. To determine your members' meeting quorum requirements, check your bylaws (and state law if you want to be sure).

Nonvoting members are usually irrelevant to your quorum needs. If you have issued nonvoting memberships or have special classes or series of memberships that are excluded from voting on particular issues, you do not normally count them when deciding whether a quorum is present.

EXAMPLE: Partners for a Better Planet has a large, loosely-structured network of contributing and volunteer members, but only 500 members hold voting memberships. The corporation ignores the nonvoting memberships in its calculation of a quorum. If 251 out of the 500 voting members attend a meeting, there is a majority quorum.

> ! **CAUTION**
>
> **Be alert to voting rules for special membership classes of shares.** If your nonprofit has a complex membership structure with different types of voting memberships, you need to establish a quorum for each class of membership for each matter submitted to the class for its approval. For example, if at an annual membership meeting, you submit a proposal to a special contributor's membership class to approve an increase to the building fund budget, you need to establish a quorum for this class at the meeting before obtaining the votes of the class on the proposal.

Some state laws and bylaws require that a quorum for members' meetings be established only once, at the beginning of the meeting. That's handy in case members representing enough voting rights (in person or by proxy) to lose a quorum leave the meeting. It allows the remaining members to nevertheless take valid, legal action. It's particularly important so that people holding a significant number of votes or proxies can't leave a meeting to prevent a vote on an item they oppose but don't have sufficient votes to stop—a tactic known as quorum-busting.

> ! **CAUTION**
>
> **Be wary of continuing business after a significant number of members leave a meeting.** If you face a controversial decision in the context of a members' meeting where you no longer have a quorum, take heed. Even if your state allows the meeting to continue, you could be inviting discord and dissent by moving forward with a decision without the participation

of the absent members. Nonprofits thrive on consensus and founder on fractionalization. To give your nonprofit the best shot at success, be as inclusive as you can when reaching membership decisions, even if it means having to convene another meeting.

Get Down to Business

Let's take a look at how a typical nonprofit conducts business at a meeting once the secretary determines that a quorum is present.

Approve Minutes from Prior Meeting

After determining that a quorum is present at the meeting, it is customary for the secretary of the meeting to read or summarize the minutes of the last meeting, The participants are then given an opportunity to vote to approve the minutes. This is an efficient way to have everyone agree that the written minutes for the prior meeting properly reflect and summarize the actions taken and decisions reached at the prior meeting. Sometimes a board member will have a minor correction to make—but this isn't the time to rehash what was discussed at the prior meeting.

TIP

Save time by getting prior approval of the minutes. No one likes long meetings. To save the trouble and boredom of reading and discussing minutes of a prior meeting, you can distribute them as part of the pre-meeting packet. Accompany it with a form that the recipient can use to indicate approval of the minutes, and a request that they mail it back or bring it with them to the next meeting. This form also provides a signed document showing that the directors or members specifically approved actions taken at a prior meeting. Especially if a director or member missed a previous meeting, it's a good idea to have this written record showing awareness and approval of important decisions reached at that earlier meeting.

Approval of Minutes

of

[name of nonprofit]

The undersigned ____[director or member]____ consents to the minutes of the __[regular, annual, or special]__ meeting of the __[directors or members]__ of _[name of nonprofit]_ held at _____[location of meeting]_____ , state of

_____ , on _____ , _____

at _____ : _____ ___ , attached to this form, and accept(s) the resolutions passed and decisions made at such meeting as valid and binding acts of the

_____

of the corporation.

Dated: _____

Signature: _____

Printed Name: _____

> **FORMS ON CD-ROM**
>
> The sample Approval of Minutes form shown above is included on the CD-ROM. (A copy of the form is also included in Appendix C.)

Hear Officer and Committee Reports

The next item on the agenda of many meetings is for the chairperson to call on committees, corporate officers, staff, and outside consultants or advisers (such as legal or tax advisers) to present or hand out presentations or reports. Reports are an excellent way to keep your board or members updated on your nonprofit's program and operations, or a particular aspect of your group's performance such as its fundraising or grant-outreach efforts. Reports not only provide a good jumping-off point for discussion at the meeting, they can also head off objections by directors or members that they were not informed on an issue.

If all the board members or members are active in the organization, presenting advisory or committee reports at the meeting may not be necessary. But when members or board members are not in day-to-day contact with the business or when there's an important decision where committee or staff analysis would help, these reports and presentations can be extremely valuable.

EXAMPLE: The Safer Streets Consortium board is considering an increase in its liability insurance to add coverage for potential liabilities related to its staff and volunteer off-site community services. Before voting on the matter, the board hears a report from a committee that had been formed to look into insurance options. The chairperson of the committee provides summaries of the cost of various coverage options from different insurance companies and makes a recommendation that the full board discusses and approves.

> **TIP**
>
> **Try to avoid presenting completely new material.** To save time at meetings, and to avoid surprise, we recommend that you provide reports and background information to directors, committee participants, and members prior to the meeting. (See Chapter 3, Step 8.) The presenters then can avoid a lengthy presentation and instead focus on the main points or participants' questions.
>
> Another good use of reports and presentations is simply to invigorate the board members' enthusiasm about the work of your nonprofit. Remember, most of these people are giving their time on a volunteer basis. If their interests flag, their participation in important tasks like fundraising or event planning might go down as well, or they might quit the board altogether. Sometimes having a staff member show up to tell a brief success story or show a few slides can make a welcome addition to the meeting.

> **TIP**
>
> **Reports can also provide legal protection for directors.** Many states have statutes that specifically immunize a director from personal liability if he or she relied on a report when reaching a decision (unless the director knew, or should have known, that the information submitted in the report was unreliable). You can use reports to help your directors feel more comfortable about making decisions without risking personal liability.

Vote on Proposals

After a report or background presentation on an issue requiring action is made, the meeting chairperson or another participant can formally introduce a proposal for discussion and vote by the directors or members. Proposals are best introduced in the form of resolutions that clearly state the item of business or matter to be approved. This allows you to include the exact language of the resolution in your minutes, with no need to reword it later. The rules about how directors and members vote on resolutions are discussed in more detail below.

> **REMINDER**
>
> **When you prepare a resolution, use short and simple language—avoid legalese.** See the examples in Chapter 3, Step 7.

Handle Unfinished Business

For one reason or another, there is often an item or two of unfinished business from the prior meeting that must be addressed at this one. Make sure you get back to the unfinished business. You should have included a summary of the unfinished business in your notice (or waiver of notice) for the current meeting.

Approving Resolutions

There are many different ways you can introduce, discuss, and approve resolutions. Typically, the chairperson or another participant at the meeting introduces a proposal on the agenda, such as whether to hire a key staff member, renew a lease for another term, or expand certain operations. The proposal can be introduced by way of a formal motion that is seconded by another participant and then discussed. Or it can simply be introduced by the chairperson with the assumption that some discussion will occur before a formal motion for a vote is made.

Either way, a discussion of the merits of the proposal is usually the next step, unless all the participants are already fully informed and ready to vote. For example, the chairperson might introduce a proposal to engage in an unrelated trade or business to generate additional revenue to support the nonprofit's activities. The board members discuss the up- and downsides of this venture, relying on a report from the group's tax-exemption and financial planning advisory committees. Once the general discussion is concluded, the chairperson can either propose adopting the resolution if one has been introduced, or propose specific language for a resolution to vote on. It's always a good idea to allow participants to voice their opinion and suggest changes to the wording of the resolution. That way you can achieve consensus and make sure you have been sensitive to all the divergent viewpoints prior to calling a vote.

After the language of a resolution is decided, the chair will ask for a vote to approve or disapprove it. If a resolution passes, it is included in the minutes of the meeting and becomes the official act of the board, committee, or membership. If it fails, it is customary to include the resolution in the minutes, noting that the resolution did not pass.

TIP

It's best to keep an exact tally of votes. For standard items of business, some nonprofits simply record in their minutes that a resolution passed by the voice vote of participants (noting that it was unanimous if all participants voiced their approval). However, for controversial or more important proposals, many make a point of specifically listing the "yea" or "nay" voice votes of each voting participant at the meeting. This attention to detail has legal and practical benefits, particularly with decisions that can have financial and legal consequences for the nonprofit. For example, a board member is unlikely to be held personally liable for a negligent or reckless board decision that causes financial harm to the nonprofit if he or she specifically voted "no" against it (instead of simply remaining silent while the rest of the board approved it). It also creates a clear record of who approved and disapproved important decisions for later reference.

Resolutions for Member Meetings

In a membership nonprofit, the board of directors usually performs most of the formal corporate decision making. The members' primary decision-making role is to elect the board of directors at the annual members' meeting. However, from time to time, the nonprofit may decide (or be required by state law) to seek membership approval of certain actions. Usually this would involve a major action or structural change to the organization, such as amending the articles of incorporation, selling or purchasing a major asset, or shifting the focus of the nonprofit's mission. When you seek member approval of a resolution, you will want to prepare members in advance and allow for a full discussion prior to taking a vote. (For more on the decision-making roles of directors and members, see "When Is Board Approval Required?" and "When Is Membership Approval (or Ratification) Required?" in Chapter 2.)

Members are not usually given any opportunity to write their own resolutions. The specific language of members' resolutions is fixed in advance by the directors at a directors' meeting. Typically, the members are mailed background material and draft resolutions prior to their meeting. At the meeting, they are simply asked to ratify the language of a resolution already proposed and approved. In some cases, reports and other background material are presented at the meeting prior to voting, and members may be asked to suggest changes to the prepared resolution. However, there usually is not as much discussion on the merits or wording of a resolution at members' meetings as there is at directors' meetings.

> **EXAMPLE:** At a special members' meeting of Disaster Relief, Inc., the members are asked to ratify an amendment to the articles of incorporation to add a new class of voting membership. The resolution presented for approval at the members' meeting is a copy of a resolution approved earlier by the board of directors. This resolution, together with a written summary of the reasons for the amendment, is sent out to the members along with notice for the meeting as part of the premeeting materials mailed to each member. (See Chapter 3, Step 8.)
>
> At the members' meeting, the resolution is introduced by the chairperson, a committee chairperson provides a report summarizing the resolution, then time is taken for

a discussion of the resolution by the members, corporate officers, and staff. Following this discussion, the chairperson makes a motion for a membership vote on the written resolution. After being seconded, the motion carries and a membership vote on the amendment is taken and recorded in the minutes of the meeting.

Voting Rules for Directors and Members

After resolutions have been presented in final form at a meeting, they must be voted on by the board of directors or members. For most resolutions, you need the majority vote of those present for the resolution to pass. Below, we summarize the state law voting rules for director and member approval of resolutions at meetings.

How the Board of Directors Votes

Unless your articles or bylaws specify otherwise, your board of directors will probably need to act by the approval of a majority of those present at the meeting. (We're assuming you already have a sufficient number of directors present to meet the quorum requirement.)

> **EXAMPLE:** A quorum of three directors attends a board meeting. The votes of two of the three directors present at the meeting are necessary to pass a resolution.

Here are some key issues that can arise during the voting process.

A director abstains. When a director abstains, it often means he or she doesn't agree to a particular action, but also doesn't want to annoy others by voting "no." In short, a director may want to duck the issue by having the minutes reflect a neutral position. That's fine, but it is important to understand that a director abstention is treated the same as a "no" vote for purposes of the vote needed to pass a resolution. Put another way, if five directors are present at a meeting, you need three "yes" votes to pass a resolution. With two "yes" votes, two "no" votes, and an abstention, the resolution fails.

Liability of silent directors. Some state statutes (and case law) say that a director can be held accountable for decisions made at meetings if the director remains silent. In other words, if the board approves a decision that was grossly negligent or unlawful and results in financial harm to the nonprofit, and someone sues, the directors who said nothing, as well as those who voted for the proposal, may be found liable for the decision. If you have doubts about a proposal submitted at your board meeting, vote "no"—don't "abstain" or remain silent as a means of expressing your disfavor. You could be held to have said "yes."

Method of voting. Unless a specific request for a written vote (ballot) is presented at the meeting, voice votes are normally fine. By the time a vote occurs, oftentimes everyone is ready to say "yes." But this isn't always the case. If there is any opposition, it's usually best to poll the board by asking each member to voice his or her vote individually and then recording each vote in the minutes. In certain situations, however, a written ballot can be useful— especially when the issue at hand is controversial or contested and participants would prefer to keep own their decisions private.

 CAUTION

Directors can't act by proxy. State law usually allows members, but not directors, to designate another person to vote at a meeting by proxy. Even if allowed, letting someone vote for a board member is risky: The absent board member could be held liable for another person's negligent or ill-advised board decisions. Bottom line for board of directors: Directors should take an active, personal interest in the decisions discussed and voted upon at board meetings, or consider resigning from the board.

How Members Vote

Under state law, each member normally has one vote. Exceptions might, however, arise if the nonprofit has established special voting classes or has adopted a special form of delegate voting—for example, voting by chapter or regional membership to elect the board.

Unlike directors, members in some organizations can vote by proxy, most likely by signing a proxy form that authorizes another person to vote on the member's behalf at a meeting. Small nonprofits don't usually allow voting by proxy, expecting that their members will be more actively involved. Instead, the members are expected to attend the meetings in person and cast their own votes. Nonprofits with a large, dispersed membership are more likely to use proxies—for example, to approve by mail the election of directors. (See Chapter 3, Step 10, for instructions on how to prepare the proxy form included on the CD-ROM.)

Unless otherwise specified in the articles or bylaws, resolutions must ordinarily be approved by a majority of the members represented at a meeting either in person or by proxy. As always, check your bylaws for your voting rules.

> **EXAMPLE:** Save All Parks has issued 10,000 voting member-ships. Members owning 8,000 memberships attend a members' meeting. That means the 5,001 quorum requirement is met (a majority of eligible voting memberships). Any action must be approved by the vote of at least 4,001 members—a majority of the voting memberships present.

Here are some issues that may come up in the course of a member vote.

Counting member abstentions. The standard voting rule under state law and bylaws is that members approve a resolution at a meeting by a majority of memberships present, with abstentions counted as "no" votes.

EXAMPLE: YouthDevelop has 100 outstanding voting memberships. Members owning 70 voting memberships attend a meeting (thus fulfilling the over-51 quorum requirement in the group's bylaws). Members with 33 memberships vote in favor of a proposal, 27 memberships vote against, and ten memberships abstain. The proposal fails because a majority of those memberships present—at least 36—did not vote in favor of the matter (all memberships not affirmatively voting "yes" are treated as "no" votes). Strangely, if the ten abstaining memberships had not attended the meeting, the proposal would have passed—a quorum of 60 memberships would have been in attendance, with a majority of the 60 memberships present (33) voting in favor of the proposal.

Check Your Articles and Bylaws for Special Voting Rules

Your articles or bylaws may require the vote of more than a majority of memberships for the approval of special types of actions. And, a greater-than-majority vote may be required under state law for certain matters such as:

- amending articles of incorporation
- dissolving the corporation after the issuance of new classes of membership, or
- selling substantially all the corporate assets.

Sometimes, the articles or bylaws give one class or series of memberships the right to a separate vote on certain proposals or to elect a board member. Make sure to check your articles and bylaws for special voting provisions.

Method of voting. Member votes are normally taken as voice votes. Or, you can use written ballots if it is more practical or you prefer it. If a member requests a polled or written vote, it is customary to allow it.

How Cumulative Voting Protects Minority Voices

With cumulative voting, each member is allowed to cast a total number of votes equal to the number of membership votes he or she holds, multiplied by the number of persons to be elected to the board. These votes can be cast all for one candidate or split up among the candidates as the member sees fit.

How does this protect minority members' interests? Let's say Abe, Ben, and Chris hold memberships that entitle each to 1,000 votes. At the annual members' meeting, four candidates are nominated for election to a three-person board. Under normal voting rules with one membership equal to one vote, Chris's candidate can always be outvoted by Abe's or Ben's choice. With cumulative voting, however, Chris is given 3,000 votes (Abe and Ben have 3,000 votes each or 6,000 together). While still outnumbered, if Chris cumulates all 3,000 votes in favor of one candidate and Abe and Ben split their votes among the other three candidates, Chris has a chance of electing her nominee to the board.

Most smaller nonprofits do not give members more than one vote per membership and do not use membership cumulative voting to elect directors unless they are required to do so—for example, if their state laws require cumulative voting to be used if a member requests it.

Election of directors. The main job of members at their annual meeting is to elect directors of the corporation for the next year. Normally, this is done by taking voice (or hand) votes or written ballots. The directors who receive the highest number of votes win—for example, the top three vote-getters from five nominees are elected to a three-person board.

But the exact procedures you'll need to follow may be more involved than this. Bylaws sometimes contain complicated provisions, based on state statutes, which specify special call, notice, and voting procedures for nominating and electing directors. Further, under state law, your articles or bylaws may require or allow cumulative voting for directors by the members—a special type of voting used primarily to protect minority member interests in larger nonprofits. And in some states, even if cumulative voting is not mentioned in the articles or bylaws, it may be requested by a member when electing the board to another term. Again, your articles and bylaws should alert you to when or whether cumulative voting must be used. Particularly if a board position is contested, you will want to be extremely careful to follow the correct procedure and may even want to double-check with a legal adviser.

Terms of office. Corporate statutes and bylaws normally require once-a-year election of directors by the members. That doesn't mean you need to elect a whole new slate of directors. Most states' laws place no limits on the number of times a person may be reelected to serve on the board.

The End: Adjourn the Meeting

After all resolutions have been submitted to a vote of the directors or members at a meeting, the chairperson should propose adjournment. If no further business is proposed and the motion carries, the meeting is adjourned.

If minutes were not prepared at the meeting, your next step is to prepare them. After they are approved at the next meeting and finalized, you'll place them in the corporate records book. We cover minutes and how to take them in the next two chapters. Place all papers presented or drafted at the meeting in the folder you prepared for the meeting or directly into your corporate records book.

TIP

Couldn't finish up? If the hour is late and you have to end the meeting with unfinished business remaining, you can schedule another meeting specifically to handle that business. The next meeting is referred to as an adjourned meeting. (For details, see Chapter 3, Step 5.) ●

5

Minutes for Directors' Annual and Special Meetings

n this chapter, we show you how to prepare minutes for directors' annual and special meetings. Keeping minutes is an important part of every nonprofit corporation's record-keeping responsibility. While there is no single proper way to prepare minutes, they should provide a clear and accurate record of the actions taken by your board.

We provide sample forms of minutes in an easy-to-use format. One is for an annual meeting of directors and the other is for a special meeting of directors. You will need to customize the forms at each meeting to suit your particular needs, but we provide instructions and examples to help you do this.

Some Basics on Minute-Taking

It is the responsibility of the corporate secretary to prepare meeting minutes. Occasionally, another person will act as secretary, but in most cases, the corporate secretary does the note-taking. Some people like to take notes by hand during the meeting and then transcribe these into minutes afterwards. If you do this, review and transcribe your notes as soon as possible after the meeting while everything is still fresh in your mind. Others prefer to use a laptop and type notes or fill in minute templates during the meeting. We recommend bringing a computer to the meeting and preparing your minutes by filling in the minutes form included on the CD-ROM in this book.

At a minimum, your minutes should provide a record of the actions taken by your board. In addition, minutes should include evidence that the board acted reasonably—for example, that the board received a report or presentation before acting on an important issue. Your minutes also should be sufficiently detailed and clear so they are useful to any reader—not just those present at the meeting. Minutes may be referred to years later by people who weren't there, and sometimes they end up in the hands of financial or tax auditors, the IRS, or even the courts.

In the sample minutes forms below, we provide language for approving standard agenda items that normally come up at an annual or special meeting of directors, such as approving the minutes from the prior meeting, establishing that a quorum is present, and—for the annual meeting—electing directors for another term.

However, you'll need to come up with your own language for less standard items of business, such as reports to the board from the finance committee or program committee. Include the name of the person who presented the report and the topic covered. Keep your description brief—use bullet points and don't include any opinions expressed by the board. Stick to a summary of what the report was about and then simply report the action taken, if any, by the board, including the votes.

Make sure you record every motion or resolution passed by the board and that you get the proper wording for the approval. Given that your nonprofit may take action or change course based on these board approvals, a formal record of these decisions is critical. With a motion, include the name of the person who made the motion and that it was seconded and passed. If you specifically refer to an agreement or document in the motion or resolution, attach a copy of the referenced material to your minutes.

It's easy to write your own resolutions and motions—simply state in simple, clear language what the board approved. There are no specific statutory legal requirements for the language of resolutions or motions. Resolutions and motions are effectively the same—they show board consideration of an item. Here are examples of the two types of wording:

- Upon motion duly made and seconded, after oral report by the CFO and board discussion, it was unanimously resolved that the organization accept federal grant #2356 in the amount of $50,000 and under the terms specified in the grant approval letter and attachments dated June 1, 2010. The secretary was asked to attach a copy of the grant approval letter and attachments along with all prior related documents, including the original and amended grant proposals, applications, and attachments, to these minutes.

- Resolved that Article 4 of the corporation's bylaws be deleted in its entirety and the following language be inserted in its place: [*insert new language here*].

Always include a statement of the voting outcome and the ultimate decision (approval or rejection) on the resolution or motion. If there are any "nay" votes or abstentions, you should list those by the voter's name. Also, be sure to record if there were any conflicts of interest declared and how the conflict was handled for voting purposes. For example, a board member might declare a family relationship with the prospective new executive director and abstain from voting to approve the hire.

Preparing Minutes for an Annual Meeting of Directors

We have provided sample minutes for a typical annual meeting of directors. You will need to customize this minutes form every time you use it, by adding the specific business items addressed at your meeting and the motions or resolutions approved. In preparing the minutes, it's often easiest to follow the agenda, using that as an outline.

Remember, your minutes serve as a factual record of what occurred at the meeting—don't include summaries of discussions, opinions expressed by board members, or details about the reports presented. Keep your minutes as short as possible, accurate, and factual, with an emphasis on action taken by your board. You can include summaries of discussions or details of report items discussed if they are central to the decisions taken or rejected.

Minutes of the Annual Meeting of Directors of (1)
[name of nonprofit]

Date: _____ (1) _____

Location: _____ (1) _____

_____ (2) _____ acted as chairperson, and

_____ (2) _____ acted as secretary of the meeting.

The meeting was called to order at _____ : _____ __ m.

The secretary announced that the meeting was held pursuant to notice properly given or that notice had been waived by directors entitled to receive notice. (3)

The secretary announced that the following directors, constituting a quorum, were present at the meeting: (4)

Present in person: (4)

_____ , _____ , _____ .

_____ , _____ , _____ .

_____ , _____ , _____ .

Present by conference call: (4)

_____ , _____ , _____ .

Absent: (4)

_____ , _____ , _____ .

The following persons were also present at the meeting:

Name	Title
(5)	

Proceedings:

Election of Directors:

The following persons were elected directors of the corporation to serve a _____ year term. **6**

_____ , _____ , _____

_____ , _____ , _____

_____ , _____ , _____ ,

_____ , _____ , _____ .

[or]

The following directors, having been elected to serve on the board for another _____ term by the members at an annual meeting of members held on _____ , _____ , accepted their positions on the board: **6**

_____ , _____ , _____

_____ , _____ , _____

_____ , _____ , _____

_____ , _____ , _____ .

The secretary announced that the presence of the directors, including the newly elected directors, represented a quorum.

The minutes from the prior directors' meeting dated **7** _____ , _____

☐ were read by the secretary.

☐ had been distributed prior to the meeting and a reading was dispensed with.

After discussion, a motion to approve the minutes was made by _____ ; seconded, and approved.

The next item of business was the appointment of committee members and others to positions in service to the corporation. After discussion, the following persons were appointed to serve on the following committees or in the service of the corporation in other capacities for the term indicated below:

Name	Committee or Role	Term
(8)		

The following reports were presented: (9)

Report: _[Name of report and person presenting report]_

[Motions, if applicable]

Report: _[Name of report and person presenting report]_

[Motions, if applicable]

Other Business: (10)

[Discussion—summary]

[Motions, if applicable]

[Discussion—summary]

[Motions, if applicable]

On motion duly made and passed, the following resolutions were adopted or rejected by the votes indicated below: **11**

_____

_____

_____

_____ .

Future Business: 12

_____

_____

_____

_____ .

There being no further business to come before the meeting, the meeting was adjourned at _____ : _____ ___ m. **13**

_____

_____ , Secretary

> **FORMS ON CD-ROM**
>
> **Above is a sample of the Minutes of the Annual Meeting of Directors form included on the CD-ROM.** Fill it out following the special instructions provided. (A copy of the form is also included in Appendix C.)

Special Instructions

1 Your minutes should always specify the type of meeting (annual, regular, special) the date and place of your meeting, and the time it was called to order and adjourned. Most annual meetings are held at the principal office of the corporation, although you are usually permitted to meet anywhere (check your bylaws).

2 Insert the names of the chairperson and secretary of the meeting. Often, the president acts as chairperson of the board and the corporate secretary of the corporation usually acts as secretary of the meeting. Under most bylaws, anyone may serve in any of these capacities, so you could appoint another director, officer, or staff person to take over if the person delegated to perform one of these tasks is absent. If that happens, state the name of the person acting in the position for the meeting.

3 Notice. Omit this statement if you didn't give notice or use written waivers of notice. Notice is usually not required for annual directors' meetings (although we recommend you always provide notice for any meeting). If you have any written waivers of notice or acknowledgments of receipt of notice, attach them to the minutes.

4 List the names of the directors present either in person or by conference call (both count as presence at the meeting). There must be a sufficient number of directors present (in person or by telephone) to represent a quorum under your bylaws.

(Remember, if you don't have a quorum, you must adjourn the meeting.) Also list the directors who are absent.

5 List any other people who are present at the meeting but don't count toward a quorum, such as staff, committee members, or the corporation's tax or legal consultant.

6 Election of directors. One of the main items of business at the annual meeting of directors is usually the election (or reelection) of directors. If you are electing directors, you will need to choose one of the two election provisions in the sample form, depending on whether you are a membership nonprofit or not.

If you don't have members, your directors will vote and elect the new directors. If you are a membership nonprofit, your directors are elected by members. At this meeting, any newly elected directors would accept their election by the members for another year. Most corporations hold their annual meeting of members just before the annual board meeting.

Include the quorum provision if the election of your new directors is effective immediately.

7 It is customary to approve the minutes from the previous meeting. Mostly this is to remind everyone of any business approved then, and to allow any objections prior to placing a copy of the minutes in the corporate records book. (We're talking about objections to what's in the minutes themselves, not to what actions were taken at the last meeting—now is not the time to bring up larger concerns like that.) Distribute copies of the minutes and have everyone read them or have the secretary read them out loud. Ask for any changes and then approve the minutes.

You can save time by sending copies of the minutes of the last meeting to the directors prior to the meeting and getting their written approval (see the Approval of Minutes form in Chapter 4). If you do this, change the minutes' approval paragraph in the sample minutes form to read as follows:

> The secretary announced that the minutes of the _[regular, annual, or special]_ directors' meeting held on ____[date]____, ____, had been distributed prior to the meeting and that each director had returned to the secretary a signed statement showing approval of the minutes of the prior meeting.

8 At the annual meeting, the board may appoint or reappoint committee members to various board committees. If your board is making appointments, list the name of each committee member being appointed, the committee to which they are being appointed, and the term of the appointment. You can also specify any other appointments made on behalf of your organization, such as a nonprofit advisory panel.

9 Reports. In this section, list (in the order presented) any reports or proposals presented to the board by officers, committee members, staff, legal advisers, or anyone else. Specify the nature of the report and the name of the person presenting the report. For example, the treasurer may give an annual financial report or the president may present the annual operations report. Document any motions or actions the board takes on a report. With motions, include the name of the person who made the motion and that it was seconded and passed.

If the board adopts or accepts a report (as written or as amended), then the report—and any motions, resolutions, or recommended actions in the report—become the act of the board. If the report is purely informational the board isn't required to take any action on it, although it may choose to accept it. Attach copies of any reports or proposals that the board accepts or adopts to your minutes and the results of the voting on it.

10 Other business. List or provide a brief summary of any other items of business that the board addresses. Include any motions or resolutions passed by the board relating to a business item.

11 Resolutions. This section is for any other resolutions or motions passed by the board. Remember, you don't need to use fancy or legal language for your resolutions or motions; just describe as specifically as you can the transaction or matter considered by your board in a short, concise statement including the votes taken and the outcome of the voting.

Here are some examples of resolutions:

Grant Example:

Upon motion duly made and seconded, and after a report by the CFO and board discussion, it was unanimously resolved that the organization accept the following grant: *[description of grant and reference to written grant terms]* .

Corporate Hiring Example:

The board unanimously approved the hiring of *[name of new employee]* , hired in the position of *[job title]* at an annual salary of $_____ and in accordance with the terms of the corporation's standard employment contract.

Tax Year Example:

After hearing an oral report from the CFO, the board discussed and unanimously decided that the corporation shall adopt a tax year with an ending date of _____ and directed the appropriate officers to file the required IRS forms.

Amendment of Articles Example:

After motion duly made and seconded, it was resolved by a majority vote that the following new article be added to the corporation's articles of incorporation [*for a membership nonprofit, add "after ratification by the members"*]: [*language of new article*]. The following directors voted against the amendment: *[list names of any "no"* _votes]_ . The following directors abstained from voting: _[list names of any abstaining directors]_ . The following directors voted "yes:" _[list names of directors who voted "yes"]_ .

If you have trouble drafting your own resolution or motion, or if the matter has important legal or tax consequences, you may wish to turn to a lawyer or accountant for help. (See Chapter 8.)

⑫ Future business. List any items that were tabled until future meetings or any assignments that board members or others took on. This will serve as an important reminder of unfinished business.

⑬ This adjournment paragraph and concluding signature line should appear at the very end of your minutes. Fill in the time the meeting ended and the name of the secretary of the meeting under the signature line.

If you are going to approve the minutes at your next meeting, the secretary can wait until after that meeting when the minutes are approved to sign them. File the final minutes in your corporate records book, together with all attachments. If you prepared a separate meeting folder to include material having to do with your meeting (such as reports, notice forms, and the like—see Chapter 3, Step 1), now is the time to transfer this material, along with your completed minutes, to your permanent corporate records book. This paperwork can come in handy later to show that your meeting was called, noticed, and held properly.

Preparing Minutes for a Special Meeting of Directors

Unlike regular or annual meetings of directors, which are scheduled in advance in your bylaws, special directors' meetings may be called during the year as needed—perhaps to discuss and vote on business items that shouldn't wait until the next scheduled meeting.

Often, these relate to important legal or tax-related matters, such as the approval of:

- a lease or real estate purchase agreement
- a bank loan or line of credit
- an amendment to articles or bylaws, or
- the issuance of a new class of membership to new or existing members, a dues increase, or a special assessment.

Sometimes, you'll need to call a special meeting of your members after the special directors' meeting, to obtain member ratification of the directors' actions. This might be required, for example, if you amend your articles of incorporation at your special directors' meeting and the amendment requires member approval.

The sample minutes form below is useful to document the actions taken at a special meeting of your directors. This form is similar to the annual directors' meeting form except that it does not contain typical annual meeting agenda items.

FORMS ON CD-ROM

Below is a sample of the Minutes of Special Meeting of Directors form included on the CD-ROM. Fill it out following any special instructions provided.

Minutes of Special Meeting of Directors of (1)

[name of nonprofit]

Date: _____ (1) _____

Location: _____ (1) _____

Purpose of meeting: ____ (1) _____ .

_____ (2) _____ acted as chairperson, and

_____ (2) _____ acted as secretary of the meeting.

The meeting was called to order at ____ (1) ____ : _____ ___ m.

The secretary announced that the meeting was called by ____ (3) _____ ;
and that it was held pursuant to notice properly given or that notice had been
waived by directors entitled to receive notice.

The secretary announced that the following directors, constituting a quorum,
were present at the meeting:

Present in person: (4)

_____ , _____ , _____

_____ , _____ , _____

_____ , _____ , _____

_____ , _____ , _____ .

Present by conference call: (4)

_____ , _____ , _____

_____ , _____ , _____ .

Absent: (4)

_____ , _____ , _____

_____ , _____ , _____ .

The following persons were also present at the meeting:

Name _____   Title _____

(5) _____   _____

_____   _____

_____   _____

Proceedings:

The chairperson called the meeting to order at _____ : _____ ___ m.

The minutes from the prior directors' meeting dated ___(6)_____ , _____

☐ were read by the secretary.

☐ had been distributed prior to the meeting and a reading was dispensed with.

After discussion, a motion to approve the minutes was made by _____

_____ ; seconded, and approved.

The following reports were presented: (7)

Report: _[Name of report and person presenting report]_____

_[Motions, if applicable]_____

Report: _[Name of report and person presenting report]_____

_[Motions, if applicable]_____

Other Business: (8)

_[Discussion—summary]_____

_[Motions, if applicable]_____

_[Discussion—summary]_____

_[Motions, if applicable]_____

On motion duly made and passed, the following resolutions were adopted or rejected by the votes indicated below: ⑨

_____

_____

_____

_____ .

Future Business: ⑩

_____

_____

_____

_____ .

There being no further business to come before the meeting, the meeting was adjourned at _____ : _____ __ m. ⑪

_____

_____ , Secretary

Special Instructions

1 Your minutes should specify that it is a special meeting of directors, the date and place of your meeting, and the time it was called to order and adjourned. Most directors' meetings are held at the principal office of the corporation, although you are usually permitted to meet anywhere (check your bylaws).

For special meetings, it's best to state the specific purpose or purposes for which the meeting was called. A similar statement of purpose should be in your notice or waiver of notice form for the meeting, although it's not always required by state law for directors' meetings.

2 Insert the names of the chairperson and secretary of the meeting. Often, the president acts as chairperson of the board and the corporate secretary of the corporation acts as secretary of the meeting. Under most bylaws, anyone may serve in any of these capacities, so you could appoint another director, officer, or staff person to take over if the person delegated to perform one of these tasks is absent. If that happens, state the name of the person acting in the position for the meeting.

3 State the name of the person who called the special meeting of directors, along with that person's title. Typically, bylaws allow the president, members of the board, a specified percentage of members, a committee chair, or others to call a special meeting of directors; check your bylaws.

Notice. Proper notice is important for special directors' meetings. You want all directors to be fully informed of the time and purpose of all specially called board meetings. Instead of providing notice, your bylaws may allow you to obtain written waivers of notice. Make sure you comply with all applicable notice requirements or obtain waivers. If you have any written waivers of notice or acknowledgments of receipt of notice, attach them to the minutes.

4 List the names of the directors present either in person or by conference call (both count as presence at the meeting). There must be a sufficient number of directors present (in person or by telephone) to represent a quorum under your bylaws. Remember, if you don't have a quorum, you must adjourn the meeting. Also list the directors who are absent.

5 List any other people who are present at the meeting and don't count toward a quorum, such as staff, committee members, or the corporation's tax or legal consultant.

6 It is customary to approve the minutes from the previous meeting. Mostly this is to remind everyone of any business approved at the last meeting and to allow any objections prior to placing a copy of the minutes in the corporate records book. Distribute copies of the minutes at the meeting and have everyone read them or have the secretary read them out loud. Ask for any changes and then approve the minutes.

You can save time by sending copies of the minutes of the last meeting to the directors prior to the meeting and getting their written approval (see the Approval of Minutes form in Chapter 4). If you do this, change the minutes' approval paragraph in the sample minutes form to read as follows:

> The secretary announced that the minutes of the _[regular, annual, or special]_ directors' meeting held on ___[date]___ , ____ , had been distributed prior to the meeting and that each director had returned to the secretary a signed statement showing approval of the minutes of the prior meeting.

7 Reports. In this section, list (in the order presented) any reports given to the board by officers, committee members, staff, legal advisors, or anyone else. Specify the nature of the report and the name of the person presenting the report. For example, the CFO may present a report on office space needs and a proposal to lease new space. If the board adopts or accepts the proposal (as written or as amended), then the proposal—and any motions, resolutions, or recommended actions in it—become the act of the board. If the report is purely informational, the board isn't required to take any action on it, although it may choose to accept it. Attach copies of any reports that the board accepts or adopts to your minutes.

8 Other business. List or provide a brief summary of any other items of business that the board addresses. Be sure to include any motions or resolutions passed by the board relating to a business item.

9 Resolutions. Document any resolutions or motions considered by the board showing whether the motion was approved or rejected and the votes taken. For example, if the purpose for the special meeting was to authorize a bank loan or amend the corporation's articles, include the board motion or resolution authorizing the action and the action taken. Make sure you get the proper wording for any action or authorization by the board.

Here are some examples of resolutions:

Bank Loan Example:

After discussion, the board unanimously resolved that the treasurer be authorized to obtain a loan from _[name of bank]_ for the amount of $_____ on terms he/she considers commercially reasonable.

Corporate Hiring Example:

The board unanimously approved the hiring of _[name of new employee]_ , hired in the position of _[job title]_ at an annual salary of $_____ and in accordance with the terms of the corporation's standard employment contract.

Tax Year Example:

After hearing an oral report from the CFO, the board discussed and unanimously decided that the corporation shall adopt a tax year with an ending date of _____ and directed the appropriate officers to file the required IRS forms.

Amendment of Articles Example:

After motion duly made and seconded, it was resolved by a majority vote that the following new article be added to the corporation's articles of incorporation [*for a membership nonprofit, add "after ratification by the members"*]: [*language of new article*]." The following directors voted against the amendment: _[list names of any "no" votes]_ . The following directors abstained from voting: _[list names of any abstaining directors]_ . The following directors voted "yes:" _[list names of directors who voted "yes"]_ .

Remember, you don't need to use fancy or legal language for your resolutions or motions; just describe as specifically as you can the transaction or matter approved by your board in a short, concise statement. If you have trouble drafting your resolution or motion, or if the matter has important legal or tax consequences, you may wish to turn to a lawyer or accountant for help.

10 Future business. List any items that were tabled until future meetings or any assignments that board members or others took on. This will serve as an important reminder of unfinished business.

11 This adjournment paragraph and concluding signature line should appear at the very end of your minutes. Fill in the time the meeting ended and the name of the secretary of the meeting under the signature line. ●

Minutes for Members' Annual and Special Meetings

n this chapter, we guide you step-by-step through the process of preparing minutes for your members' annual and special meetings. Included are two sample forms—one for an annual meeting and one for a special meeting, which you'll learn to customize to suit your particular needs.

Some Basics on Minute-Taking

It's normally the responsibility of the corporate secretary to prepare meeting minutes. Occasionally, you may need to ask another person to act as secretary of the meeting but in most cases, the corporate secretary does the note-taking.

Some people like to take notes by hand during the meeting and then transcribe the notes into meeting minutes afterwards. If you do this, be sure to review and transcribe your notes as soon as possible after the meeting while everything is still fresh in your mind. Others prefer to use a laptop and type notes or prepare the minutes at the meeting. We recommend bringing a computer to the meeting and preparing your minutes by filling in the minutes form included on the CD-ROM in this book.

The sample minutes forms below provide language for approving standard items of business. For a member's annual meeting, the main item of business is usually the election of directors. Special meetings, on the other hand, are usually called to obtain member approval for a particular matter. For example, the board may have approved an amendment to the articles of incorporation and now seeks member ratification of the amendment.

Make sure you record every action, motion, or resolution passed by your members and that you get the proper wording for the approval. You can state that the motion or resolution was duly made and seconded, and state the name of the persons who made the motion and seconded it. If that sounds too formal, it's okay to repeat the wording of the motion or resolution approved or rejected, and include the votes taken for or against it. If you refer to an agreement or document in the motion or resolution, attach a copy of it to your minutes. It's easy to write your own resolutions and motions—you simply state in simple, clear language exactly what the members approved.

Preparing Minutes for an Annual Meeting of Members

The sample minutes form in this book will help you fulfill your obligations for a typical annual meeting of members. Customize this form by adding the specific business items addressed at your meeting and the specific motions or resolutions approved by your members. In preparing the minutes, it's often easiest to follow the agenda, using that as an outline.

Remember, your minutes serve as a factual record of what occurred at the meeting—but there's no need to create a word-for-word transcription. Keep your minutes as short as possible, accurate, and factual with an emphasis on action taken by your members. Don't include opinions expressed or details about discussions or reports presented.

FORMS ON CD-ROM

Below is a sample of the Minutes of Annual Meeting of Members form included on the CD-ROM. Fill it out following the special instructions provided. (A copy of the form is also included in Appendix C.)

Minutes of Annual Meeting of Members of ①

[name of nonprofit]

Date: ① _____

Location: ① _____

Purpose: To elect directors and for the transaction of any other business that may properly come before the meeting, including ① _____

_____ .

② _____ acted as chairperson, and
② _____ acted as secretary of the meeting.

The meeting was called to order at _____ : _____ m.

The secretary announced that the meeting was called by ③ _____ .

The secretary announced that the meeting was held pursuant to notice properly given or that notice had been waived by all members entitled to receive notice. ④

The secretary announced that an alphabetical list of the names and, if appropriate, type of membership interests held by all members of the nonprofit corporation was available and open to inspection by any person in attendance at the meeting.

Proceedings:

The secretary announced that the following members, constituting a quorum, were present in person or by proxy: ⑤

Name	Proxyholder, if any
⑥ _____	_____
_____	_____
_____	_____
_____	_____
_____	_____
_____	_____

The secretary attached written proxy statements, executed by the appropriate members, to these minutes for any members listed above represented by a proxyholder.

The following persons were also present at the meeting:

Name _____   Title _____

(7) _____   _____

_____   _____

_____   _____

The minutes from the prior members' meeting dated __(8)_____ , _____

☐ were read by the secretary.

☐ had been distributed prior to the meeting and a reading was dispensed with.

After discussion, a motion to approve the minutes was made by _____
_____ ; seconded, and approved.

Election of Directors (9)

The chairperson announced that the next item of business was the nomination and election of the board of directors for another _____ term of office. The following nominations were made and seconded:

Names of Nominees _____

_____

_____

_____

_____

_____

_____

_____

_____

The secretary next took the votes of members entitled to vote for the election of directors at the meeting. After counting the votes, the secretary announced that the following persons were elected to serve on the board of directors of this corporation for another term:

Name _____ Term _____

_____ _____

_____ _____

_____ _____

_____ _____

_____ _____

_____ _____

The following reports were presented: (10)

Report: _[Name of report and person presenting report]_____

_[Motions, if applicable]_____

Report: _[Name of report and person presenting report]_____

_[Motions, if applicable]_____

Other Business: (11)

_[Discussion—summary]_____

_[Motions, if applicable]_____

_[Discussion—summary]_____

_[Motions, if applicable]_____

On motion duly made and passed, the following resolutions were adopted or rejected by the votes of members present in person or by proxy as indicated below: (12)

_____

_____

_____

_____ .

There being no further business to come before the meeting, the meeting was adjourned at _____ : _____ __ m. (13)

_____

_____ , Secretary

Special Instructions

① Your minutes should always specify the type of meeting (annual, biennial, special). Most state statutes and most nonprofits' bylaws call for the annual election of directors by the members. However, if your bylaws allow you to hold elections less frequently—say, every two years—then change the word "annual" in the heading to "biennial" (and make the same change throughout the text).

State the date and place of the meeting, and the time it was called to order and adjourned. Members' meetings are often held at the principal office of the corporation, although you are usually permitted to meet anywhere (check your bylaws).

Purpose. You can list any matters, other than the election of directors, which will be considered at the meeting. You are not required to do this—the text in the sample form authorizes the transaction of any other business that may come before the meeting. But most nonprofits list all significant items that will be addressed at the meeting.

② Insert the names of the chairperson and secretary of the meeting. Your bylaws may specify who should act as chairperson of members' meetings. Sometimes it is the president or, in his or her absence, the vice president or another executive officer. Usually the corporate secretary of the corporation acts as secretary of the meeting. Under most bylaws, anyone may serve in any of these capacities, so you could appoint another director, officer, or staff person to take over if the person delegated to perform one of these tasks is absent. If that happens, state the name of the person acting in the position for the meeting.

In the instructions for this form, we specify when we are referring to the secretary of the nonprofit corporation. All other references are to the secretary of the meeting. Normally, the secretary of the corporation and the secretary of the meeting will be one and the same.

3 This is an optional provision. Often, annual members' meetings are not officially "called," because they are already scheduled in the bylaws. (See Chapter 3, Step 3, for a discussion of the legal requirements for calling meetings.) If your nonprofit follows a different practice and you wish to show that the secretary of the corporation, another officer or board member, or a number of members called the meeting, include this paragraph. Indicate the name and title of each person who called the meeting.

4 Notice. For members' meetings, we recommend providing written notice prior to the meeting. If you own and run a small nonprofit with a small number of active directors and members, you may decide to use waiver of notice forms. If you have any written waivers of notice or acknowledgments of receipt of notice, attach them to the minutes.

5 Usually you must make available at member meetings an alphabetical list of all members. You can prepare a separate meeting participant list (as explained in Chapter 3, Step 4), or simply make your corporate records book available for inspection at the meeting. If you use your corporate records book, it must include a membership roster with a current listing of your members and their membership interests. If each member has one vote, you don't usually have to specify the voting rights. But if there are different classes of memberships with different voting rights, the roll or register should list each member's class of membership and the number of votes or voting power granted to each member.

6 List the names of the members present at the meeting. To the right of each name, if any member is represented at the meeting by proxy, list the name of the proxyholder. Attach copies of each written proxy to the minutes.

REMINDER

No quorum, no action. Remember that most bylaws require that a majority of the voting members of the corporation attend the meeting in order to reach a quorum.

7 List any people, other than the chairperson and secretary of the meeting, who attend the meeting but do not count toward a quorum. For example, officers, staff or committee members may be there to give reports to members, and there may be others in attendance such as other board members or the corporation's tax, legal, or financial consultant.

8 It is customary, though not legally necessary, for participants at meetings to approve the minutes of the previous meeting. However, if your last meeting was held a year ago, you may want to dispense with this formality (and delete this paragraph). You have probably already placed a copy of the minutes in your corporate records and it's unlikely that anyone will remember the details of a meeting held a year ago.

If you decide to follow this formality, distribute copies of the minutes at the meeting and have everyone read them or have the secretary read them out loud. Ask for any changes and then approve the minutes.

Or, you can save time by sending copies of the minutes of the last meeting to the members prior to the meeting and getting their written approval (see Chapter 4 for the Approval of Minutes form). If you do this, change the minutes' approval paragraph in the sample minutes form to read as follows:

The secretary announced that the minutes of the __[regular, annual, or special]__ members' meeting held on ____[date]____ , had been distributed prior to the meeting and that each member had returned to the secretary a signed statement showing approval of the minutes of the prior meeting.

9 Election of directors. Here you take care of the main business of the annual members' meeting—the election (or reelection) of the directors of your corporation for another term of office. Indicate the term of office in the first blank. Most bylaws provide for a one year (annual) term, although occasionally bylaws specify a longer term. Under "Name of Nominee," fill in the names of all nominees who are to be voted upon by the members. Many small nonprofits simply nominate (and reelect) each member of the current board for another term of office. But check your bylaws, and make sure to provide a fair procedure by which each member or membership class has a chance to place one or more names in nomination. In other words, don't simply nominate the directors currently sitting on the board without giving your members a chance prior to or at the meeting to suggest others. Your bylaws should contain any requirements imposed under state law for the nomination and election of directors.

Corporate statutes usually allow corporations to provide for a classified or staggered board in their bylaws. Typically, this means that the board is broken down—or classified—into two or more groups, with the elections for each section scheduled for alternate years.

EXAMPLE:

The Child Protection Project, Inc., has a nine-member board, and its bylaws provide for one-third of the board to be reelected every three years. At each annual members' meeting, one-third of the board is replaced or reelected to serve another three-year term.

In these blanks, say who has been elected to serve on the board for another term.

Normal voting procedures. Most nonprofit corporations elect directors by voice vote or written ballot, and elect those nominees who receive the most votes. In some nonprofits with broad membership classes made up of different interest group, the articles or bylaws may call for cumulative voting procedures. (We discuss member voting rules in more detail in Chapter 4.)

EXAMPLE:

Ten members, with one vote per membership, vote for three of five nominees to a three-person board (each member may cast a vote in favor of each of three candidates). There are a total of 30 possible votes. The results are as follows:

	Number of Votes Cast	Result in Favor of Candidate
Nominee 1	10	Elected
Nominee 2	10	Elected
Nominee 3	5	Elected
Nominee 4	3	Not Elected
Nominee 5	2	Not Elected

In the above example, Nominees 1 and 2 received the votes of all ten members, while Nominees 3, 4, and 5 received the votes of five, three, and two members respectively. The three candidates receiving the largest number of votes, Nominees 1, 2, and 3, are elected to the board.

10 Reports. Officers, staff, or others may present annual or special reports at the meeting. For example, an executive officer may give an annual operating report, and the treasurer may summarize the past year's program, fundraising, and fund balance results and figures. List a description of the reports given, such as "treasurer's fund balance report," along with the name and title of the presenter. Attach any written copies of reports to your minutes.

11 Other business. Use this space for any other business that comes up at the meeting.

12 Resolutions. In addition to the election of directors, members are sometimes asked to vote on proposals at the annual meeting. For example, the members may be asked to ratify an amendment to the nonprofit corporation's articles. Use this section to show the vote on the resolution and include the language of the resolution as approved by the members. Member resolutions normally must be passed by a majority of those attending and entitled to vote—check your bylaws. If you pass a resolution that requires a different vote requirement under your bylaws, you should precede the text of the resolution with a statement that the resolution was passed by the appropriate number or percentage of votes.

You don't need to use fancy or legal language for your resolution; just describe as specifically as you can the transaction or matter considered by your members in a short, concise statement. Make sure you accurately state any action or authorization by your members or get the correct wording for any resolution passed. Indicate the votes taken and the outcome of the voting (approval or rejection or abstention).

Traditionally, resolutions start with a preamble of the following sort: "The members resolved that...," but this is not required.

Here are a few examples of resolutions:

Amendment of Articles Example:

The members unanimously ratified a board of directors' resolution adding the following new article to the corporation's articles of incorporation: [*language of new article*].

Amendment of Bylaws Example:

The members approved by the votes indicated below an amendment to the bylaws of the corporation. The text of the changed bylaws is as follows: [*language of amended bylaws*]." State the tally of membership votes for, against, or abstaining.

If you have trouble drafting your own resolution, or if the matter has important legal or tax consequences, you may wish to turn to a lawyer or accountant for help.

13 This concluding adjournment paragraph and signature line should appear at the very end of your minutes. Fill in the name of the secretary of the meeting under the signature line.

After the secretary signs, file the completed minutes in your corporate records book together with all attachments.

If you prepared a separate meeting folder for the meeting, now is the time to transfer all forms and attachments related to the meeting from the folder to your corporate records book.

Preparing Minutes for a Special Meeting of Members

You may call special meetings during the year to discuss and vote on special items of business that have come up between regularly scheduled meetings, and that need member approval. Typically, the board of directors calls the member meeting to ratify its actions or to obtain approval of a matter on which the board cannot act independently (such as the amendment of articles).

State corporate statutes usually require the approval by members of important structural changes to the corporation or of matters in which the directors have a direct financial interest (such as the approval of a loan or guaranty to a director or officer). A special members' meeting might be called to ratify an amendment to the articles, to authorize issuing additional classes of membership, or to dissolve the nonprofit corporation.

Of course, the members themselves may call a special membership meeting, or the board may decide to call one, simply to discuss and approve an important nonprofit program or financial decision. Even if member approval isn't legally required, the directors may decide to call a special members' meeting to ask for ratification of a decision already made by the board. Consensus among members is, after all, important for maintaining community involvement in a nonprofit.

In these cases, most of the groundwork for preparing the minutes, including the drafting of resolutions to present to the special members' meeting, will already have been done as part of the process of holding the prior board meeting and preparing the minutes for it.

REMINDER

Have you made sure people know about the meeting? As discussed in Chapter 2, you'll need to call and provide notice for all special members' meetings as provided in your bylaws, unless you've had each member sign a written waiver of notice form prior to the meeting.

FORMS ON CD-ROM

Below is a sample of the Minutes of Special Meeting of Members form included on the CD-ROM. (A copy of the form is also included in Appendix C.)

Minutes of Special Meeting of Members of

[name of nonprofit]

Date: _____ **(1)** _____

Location: _____ **(1)** _____

Purpose of meeting: _____ **(2)** _____

_____

_____ **(3)** _____ acted as chairperson, and

_____ acted as secretary of the meeting.

The meeting was called to order at _____ **(1)** : _____ __ m.

The secretary announced that the meeting was called by _____ **(4)** _____ ;
and that it was held pursuant to notice properly given or that notice had been
waived by members entitled to receive notice.

The secretary announced that an alphabetical list of the names and, if appropriate,
type of membership interest, held by all members of the corporation was
available and open to inspection by any person in attendance at the meeting. **(5)**

The secretary announced that there were present, in person or by proxy,
representing a quorum of the members, the following members:

Name	Proxyholder, if any
(6)	

The secretary attached written proxy statements, executed by the appropriate members, to these minutes for any members listed above represented by a proxyholder.

The following persons were also present at the meeting:

Name   Title

(7)

_____   _____

_____   _____

_____   _____

_____   _____

_____   _____

_____   _____

_____   _____

_____   _____

Proceedings: **(8)**

The minutes from the prior members' meeting dated _____ , _____

☐ were read by the secretary.

☐ had been distributed prior to the meeting and a reading was dispensed with.

After discussion, a motion to approve the minutes was made by _____

_____ ; seconded, and approved.

The following reports were presented: **(9)**

Report: _[Name of report and person presenting report]_____

_[Motions, if applicable]_____

Report: _[Name of report and person presenting report]_____

_[Motions, if applicable]_____

Other Business: (10)

[Discussion—summary]

[Motions, if applicable]

[Discussion—summary]

[Motions, if applicable]

On motion duly made and passed, the following resolutions were adopted or rejected by the votes of members present in person or by proxy as indicated below: (11)

There being no further business to come before the meeting, the meeting was adjourned at ____ : ____ __ m. (12)

_____, Secretary

Special Instructions

1 Insert the date, time, and place (street address, city, and state) of the meeting. Members' meetings are usually held at the principal office of the corporation, although most bylaws allow these meetings to be held anywhere.

2 List the specific purpose or purposes for which the special members' meeting was called. State law usually prohibits the transaction of any business not specified in the notice or waiver of notice for a special members' meeting. A similar statement of purpose should have been included in your notice or waiver of notice form for the meeting.

Sample statements of purpose of special meetings include:

"to ratify an amendment to the articles of incorporation already approved by the board of directors that provides for the creation of a new class of membership," or

"to approve an amendment to the bylaws of the corporation already approved by the board of directors that increases the minimum quorum requirement for members' meetings."

3 Insert the name and title of the persons who acted as chairperson and secretary of the meeting. Bylaws often provide that the president or chairperson of the board presides at meetings of members, and the corporate secretary acts as secretary of meetings of members.

In the instructions for this form, we specify when we are referring to the secretary of the nonprofit corporation. All other references are to the secretary of the meeting. The secretary of the corporation and the secretary of the meeting often will be one and the same.

4 Indicate who called the special meeting of members. It may have been more than one person. Also include each person's title. Typically, bylaws and state law allow the board of directors, the president, or a minimum of 10% of the members to call a special meeting of members. (See Chapter 3, Step 3, and check your bylaws.)

4 Proper notice or waiver of notice is important for special members' meetings. After all, you don't want an uninformed member to complain later and challenge a decision. This paragraph states that each member was given notice as required by your bylaws, or waived notice by signing a written waiver form.

Attach to your minutes any acknowledgments of receipt or written waivers of notice for the meeting that were signed by members.

5 Usually you must make available at member meetings an alphabetical list of all members of your nonprofit. You can prepare a separate meeting participant list (as explained in Chapter 3, Step 4), or you can simply make your corporate records book available for inspection at the meeting. If you use your corporate records book, it must include a membership roster with a current listing of your members and their membership interests. If each member has one vote, you don't usually have to specify the voting rights. But if there are different classes of memberships with different voting rights, the roll or register should list each member's name and the class of membership and the number of votes or voting power granted to each member.

6 List the names of the members present at the meeting. If any member is represented at the meeting by proxy, list the name of the proxyholder to the right of the member's name. Attach copies of each written proxy to the minutes.

REMINDER

Special meetings are no excuse to ignore quorum requirements. Most bylaws require that a majority of the voting members of the corporation attend the special meeting for a quorum to be reached.

7 Specify any additional persons, other than the chairperson and secretary of the meeting, who attended the meeting but do not count toward a quorum. For example, if officers, staff, or committee members present reports to the members, they should be listed here, as well as any board members who attended, and the nonprofit's tax, legal, or financial consultants.

8 It is customary, though not legally necessary, for participants at meetings to approve the minutes of the previous meeting. However, if your last meeting was held a year ago, you may want to dispense with this formality (and delete this paragraph). You have probably already placed a copy of the minutes in your corporate records and it's unlikely that anyone will remember the details of a meeting held a year ago.

If you decide to follow this formality, distribute copies of the minutes at the meeting and have everyone read them or have the secretary read them out loud. Ask for any changes and then approve the minutes.

Or, you can save time by sending copies of the minutes of the last meeting to the members prior to the meeting and getting their written approval (see Chapter 4 for the Approval of Minutes form). If you do this, change the minutes' approval paragraph in the sample minutes form to read as follows:

> The secretary announced that the minutes of the __*[regular, annual, or special]*__ members' meeting held on ____*[date]*___, ____, had been distributed prior to the meeting and that each member had returned to the secretary a signed statement showing approval of the minutes of the prior meeting.

9 Reports. There may be officers, staff, committees, or others who present reports at the meeting. Specify the nature of each report (such as treasurer's fund balance report) and the name and title of the person submitting it. Attach any written copies of reports to your minutes.

10 Other business. Use this space for any other business that comes up at the meeting.

11 Resolutions. Here you take care of the main business of a special members' meeting—the consideration and approval or rejection of one or more resolutions by the members in attendance. Use this section to show the members' vote on the resolution and include the language of the resolution.

Member resolutions normally must be passed by a majority of those attending and entitled to vote at a meeting—check your bylaws. If you pass a resolution that went by different voting rules as required under your bylaws, precede the text of the resolution with a statement that the resolution was passed by whatever number or percentage of votes was appropriate.

List all the resolutions that were considered and voted upon at the meeting. Often, members will be asked to ratify a board decision, such as an amendment of the articles already approved by the directors. However, they can also act independently to approve certain matters on their own—for example, the amendment of bylaws. Make sure you accurately state any action or authorization by your members and get the correct wording for any resolution passed.

You don't need to use fancy or legal language for your resolution; just describe as specifically as you can the transaction or matter considered by your members in a short, concise statement and include the outcome of the voting. You can use a preamble at the beginning of your resolutions such as: "The members resolved that…," but this is not required.

Here are some examples of resolution language:

Amendment of Articles Example:

The members unanimously ratified a board of directors' resolution adding the following new articles to the corporation's articles of incorporation: [*language of new articles*].

Amendment of Bylaws Example:

The members approved by the votes listed below an amendment to the bylaws of the corporation. The text of the changed bylaws is as follows: [*language of amended bylaws*]." [*Indicate the tally of membership votes for, against, and abstaining.*]

If you have trouble drafting your own resolution language, or if the matter has important legal or tax consequences, you may wish to turn to a lawyer or accountant for help.

⑫ This concluding adjournment paragraph and signature line should appear at the very end of your minutes, after any resolutions. Fill in the name of the secretary of the meeting under the signature line. After the minutes are finalized and signed by your secretary, file them in your corporate records book together with all attachments.

If you prepared a separate meeting folder for the special meeting, now is the time to transfer all forms and attachments related to the meeting from your folder to your corporate records book. ●

How to Take Action by Written Consent

Meetings are good for considering options, sharing ideas, and allowing open discussion and debate. But there may be times when you can't get everyone together or it simply doesn't make sense to call a meeting for one discrete non-controversial matter that has come up. Instead of holding a meeting, you can use written consent forms which directors or members sign authorizing an action or approving a decision. This is much easier and less time-consuming than holding a meeting.

Written consents are most appropriate for small nonprofit corporations with only a few members or directors. With only a few people running a nonprofit, there is probably ample opportunity for those people to talk over issues that arise. They may find it easier to simply document certain decisions with written consents than separately notice and hold a meeting.

With larger organizations, try to avoid using written consents except in extenuating circumstances—for example, if you have a deadline for making a decision and there isn't time to assemble your board or members at a special meeting.

In all cases, action by written consent is most appropriate if the issue at hand is a routine tax, program, or financial formality; for instance, the approval of standard loan terms for a loan or the approval of a tax election recommended by your accountant. It is not appropriate where a decision could involve debate or disagreement among directors or members.

TIP

Another handy use for written consents. If a director or member can't attend a meeting where important decisions are being voted on, it's a good idea to have that person sign a consent form. This is true even if you don't need the absent director or member's consent to legally approve the matter. You'll ensure that all directors or members are informed of actions being taken and create clear evidence of their assent to the decision.

Check Your Written Consent Rules

If you plan on using written consents for your directors or members, start by checking your bylaws and state law to determine what rules you must follow. Most state nonprofit statutes lay out specific rules for written consents. The most common requirement is that any action done by written consent by directors or members must be *unanimous*. Some states, however, allow less than unanimous consent for certain member approvals, as explained in more detail below.

Written Consent Rules for Directors

Most states have a statute specifically authorizing director action by written consent. Usually, the written consent of all directors is required. But if you think that one or more directors may object to the action or resolution at hand, then you will need to hold a meeting.

Written Consent Rules for Members

Most states allow member action by written consent. A majority of states require unanimous member consent. In other words, all members entitled to vote on a matter must actually sign the consent form for it to pass.

Some states allow written approval by less than the unanimous consent of members. They may, for example, set the required number or percentage of members who sign written consents as equal to what would be required if the members were actually voting at a meeting with all members present. Other states (following the Revised Model Nonprofit Act) allow 80% of the members to take action by written consent.

However, even in states that allow less than unanimous written consent, certain member actions, such as a change in membership rights or obligations, may still require the unanimous written approval of members. Or you may live in a state that allows less than unanimous written consent by members in all matters except the election of directors. Check your bylaws and state law for the written consent rules in your state.

> **CAUTION**
>
> **There's safety in unanimity.** We recommend that you always obtain the unanimous written consent of your directors or members. Doing so not only ensures that you will meet the most stringent bylaw and state law requirements, but also gives notice to everyone who'd normally participate in the decision and puts their assent on record.

Prepare the Written Consent Form

Below is a sample of the Written Consent to Action Without Meeting form included on the enclosed CD-ROM. Fill it out following the special instructions provided. (A copy of the form is also included in Appendix C.)

Written Consent to Action Without Meeting

The undersigned _[directors or members]_ **1** of _[name of nonprofit corporation]_ hereby consent as follows:

2 _____

_____

_____

_____

_____

_____

_____

_____ .

Dated: **3** _____

Signature: _____   Printed Name _____

3 _____   _____

_____   _____

_____   _____

_____   _____

_____   _____

_____   _____

_____   _____

_____   _____

_____   _____

Special Instructions

(1) Indicate whether the consent form is for directors or members of your nonprofit corporation. If you want both the directors and members to approve a given action, prepare separate forms.

(2) Insert a description of the actions or decisions to be approved by the written consent of the directors or members. You don't need to use fancy or legal language for the decision or action under consideration—just describe it as specifically as you can in a short, concise statement using simple, straightforward language. Here are some examples:

Bank Loan Example:

> The board hereby authorizes the treasurer be authorized to obtain a loan from _[name of bank]_ for the amount of $ _____ on terms [he/she] considers commercially reasonable.

Corporate Hiring Example:

> The board approves the hiring of _[name of new employee]_ , to be hired in the position of _[job title]_ at an annual salary of $ _____ and in accordance with the terms of the corporation's standard employment contract.

Tax Year Example:

> The board hereby decides that the corporation shall adopt a tax year with an ending date of March 31 and directs the appropriate officers to file the required IRS forms.

Amendment of Articles Example:

> The members whose signatures appear below approve the addition of the following new article to the corporation's articles of incorporation: _[title and language of new article]_ .

If you have trouble drafting the language for your written consent or if the matter has important legal or tax consequences, you may wish to turn to a lawyer or accountant for help.

(3) Date the consent form and have your directors or members sign their names. If you have only a few directors or members, you could prepare one master consent form and pass it around to your directors or members to sign. In that case, date the form as of the date of the first signature by a director or member. Another method, more appropriate when you have a larger number of directors or members, is to prepare a separate consent form that each director or member would date and sign. Either method works.

Place Signed Consent Forms in Your Corporate Records Book

After distributing your written consents and obtaining the signatures of your directors or members, place each completed form in your corporate records book. It's common to place these papers in the minutes section of the corporate records book, arranged according to the date the consent was signed. ●

Help Beyond This Book

Much of the work in holding nonprofit meetings and documenting decisions is routine. For the most part, any knowledgeable and motivated person can do it. But from time to time you're bound to need help from outside sources. You will undoubtedly run into questions concerning law or taxes where an expert's advice will be well worth the fee. In this chapter, we provide a few tips to help you in your search for competent expert information, assistance, and advice.

How to Find the Right Lawyer

Most small nonprofits can't afford to put a lawyer on retainer. Even when consulted on an issue-by-issue basis, lawyers' fees mount up fast—way too fast to be affordable to most smaller organizations. More and more small nonprofits are trying to close this affordability gap by doing as much of their own legal research and work as possible. Often a knowledgeable self-help staffperson or board member can sensibly accomplish the whole task. (However, you can't expect a board member who's a lawyer to have all the answers, especially if he or she specializes in, say, immigration law or criminal defense.) Other times, it makes sense to briefly consult with a lawyer at an interim stage or have your paperwork reviewed upon completion.

You've already taken one positive step toward making your legal life affordable by using this book to help you prepare standard minutes and written consent forms. Depending on the size of your nonprofit and the complexity of your legal needs, your next step is likely to be to find a cooperative lawyer—one who's willing, for example, to review the legal ramifications of a potential decision and review or draft specific resolutions for your board or members approval.

You obviously don't want a lawyer who is programmed to try and take over all your legal decision making and drafting while running up billable hours as fast as possible. Instead, you need what we call a legal coach, someone who is willing to work with you—not just for you. Under this model, the lawyer works to help you take care of many routine legal matters yourself, and is also available to consult on more complicated legal issues as the need arises.

TIP

You don't need a big-time business lawyer. There is a lawyer surplus these days, and many newer lawyers, in particular, are open to nontraditional business arrangements. Look for a lawyer with significant nonprofit experience (it is an area in which some lawyers specialize). Avoid lawyers who work only with business corporations. Not only will they deal mostly with issues that are remote from your concerns, but they're almost sure to charge too much.

TIP

Don't ask a lawyer for tax advice. When it comes to making decisions that have tax implications, tax advisers usually have a better grasp of the issues than lawyers. And an added bonus is that although tax advice doesn't come cheap, tax advisers sometimes charge less than lawyers.

Look and Ask Around

When you go looking for a lawyer, talk to people in your community who operate similar nonprofits. Ask them about their lawyer and what they think of that person's work and fees. If you talk to half a dozen nonprofit people, chances are you'll come away with several good leads. Nonprofit resource centers may be able to provide the names of lawyers who specialize in nonprofit representation and problem-solving. Friends, relatives, and associates within your own personal network may also have names of possible nonprofit lawyers. You can also check Nolo's lawyer directory at www.nolo. com to see if there are any nonprofit lawyer listings in your area.

TIP

Let your legal coach refer you to experts when necessary. What if you have a very technical legal question? Should you start by seeking out a legal specialist? For starters, the answer is probably no. First, find a good nonprofit lawyer to act as your coach. Then rely on this person to suggest other experts as the need arises.

Talk to the Lawyer Ahead of Time

After you get the names of several good prospects, don't wait until two days before an important meeting or until you're deep in a legal crisis before contacting a lawyer. By that point, you may not have time to find a lawyer who will work with you at affordable rates. Chances are you'll wind up settling for the first person available at a moment's notice—almost a guarantee you'll pay too much for poor service.

When you call a lawyer, announce your intentions in advance— that you are looking for someone who is willing to review your papers from time to time, point you in the right direction as the need arises, serve as a legal adviser as circumstances dictate, and tackle legal problems if they arise. In exchange, let the lawyer know you are willing to pay promptly and fairly. If the lawyer seems agreeable to this arrangement, ask to come in to meet for a half hour or so. Many lawyers will not charge you for this introductory appointment.

At the interview, reemphasize that you are looking for a nontraditional legal coach relationship. Many lawyers will find this unappealing—for example, saying they don't feel comfortable reviewing documents you've drafted using self-help materials. If so, thank the person for being frank, and keep interviewing other lawyers. You'll also want to discuss other important issues in this initial interview, such as the lawyer's customary charges for services, as explained further below.

Pay particular attention to the rapport between you and your lawyer. Remember—you are looking for a legal coach who will work with you. Trust your instincts and seek a lawyer whose personality and outlook are compatible with your own. It often helps to find a lawyer who is interested in your nonprofit mission and program goals.

Set the Extent and Cost of Services in Advance

Before hiring a lawyer, get a clear understanding about how fees will be computed. For example, if you call the lawyer from time to time for general advice or to be steered to a good information source, how will you be billed? Some lawyers bill a flat amount for a call or a conference; others bill to the nearest six-, ten-, or 20-minute interval. Whatever the lawyer's system, you need to understand it.

Especially at the beginning of your relationship, when you bring a big job to a lawyer, ask specifically what it will cost. If you feel it's too much, don't hesitate to negotiate; perhaps you can do some of the routine work yourself, thus reducing the fee.

It's a good idea to get all fee arrangements—especially those for good-sized jobs—in writing. In several states, fee agreements between lawyers and clients must be in writing if the expected fee is $1,000 or more or is contingent on the outcome of a lawsuit. But whether legally required or not, putting your agreement in writing helps avoid unpleasant surprises and misunderstandings.

How Lawyers Charge for Legal Services

There are no across-the-board arrangements for how lawyers' fees are computed. Expect to be charged by one of the following methods:

- **By the hour.** In most parts of the United States, you can get competent legal services for $200 to $250 an hour. Newer attorneys still in the process of building a practice may be available for paperwork review, legal research, and other types of work at lower rates. Also, a nonprofit lawyer who is committed to your nonprofit mission and goals may agree to charge you less than their going rate. Some may even agree to provide pro bono work (free) for your organization or agree to sit on your board and/or act as corporate legal secretary, preparing minutes and consents for your nonprofit.

- **Flat fee for a specific job.** Under this arrangement, you pay the agreed-upon amount for a given project, regardless of how much or how little time the lawyer spends. Particularly when you first begin working with a lawyer and are worried about hourly costs getting out of control, negotiating a flat fee for a specific job can provide predictability and reassurance.

- **Contingent fee based upon settlement amounts or winnings.** This type of fee typically occurs in personal injury, products liability, fraud, and discrimination type cases, where a lawsuit has been filed. The lawyer gets a percentage of the recovery (often 33%–40%) if you win and nothing if you lose. Since most nonprofit legal work involves advice and help with drafting paperwork, a contingency fee approach doesn't normally make sense.

- **Retainer.** Some nonprofits can afford to pay relatively modest amounts, perhaps $1,000 to $5,000 a year, to keep a lawyer on retainer for ongoing phone or in-person consultations, routine premeeting minutes review, or resolution preparation and other matters during the year. Of course, your retainer won't cover a full-blown legal crisis, but it can help you take care of ongoing minutes and other legal paperwork when you need a hand.

TIP

Nonlawyer professionals can help you cut down on legal costs. For example, look to nonprofit consultants for program planning and compliance, real estate brokers or appraisers for valuation of properties, financial planners for nonprofit fund investment advice, tax advisers for preparation of financial proposals, insurance agents for advice on insurance protection, independent paralegals for routine corporate resolution or form drafting, and CPAs for audit work and preparation of tax returns. Each of these matters is likely to have a legal aspect, and you may eventually want to consult your lawyer; but normally you won't need to until you've gathered information on your own.

Confront Any Problems Head-On

If you have any questions about a lawyer's bill or the quality of services, speak up. Buying legal help should be just like purchasing any other consumer service—if you are dissatisfied, you can request a reduction in your bill or make it clear that the work needs to be redone properly. If the lawyer runs a decent business, he or she will promptly and positively deal with your concerns. If you don't get an acceptable response, find another lawyer pronto. If you switch lawyers, you are entitled to get your important documents back from the first lawyer.

Even if you fire your lawyer, you may still feel wronged. If you can't get satisfaction from the lawyer, write to the client grievance office of your state bar association (with a copy sent to the lawyer, of course). Often, a phone call from this office to your lawyer will bring the desired results.

How to Find the Right Tax Adviser

Many nonprofit corporate resolutions and ongoing corporate decisions involve tax issues and advice (such as tax-exemption compliance and reporting issues). To make good decisions in these and other complicated areas may require the expert advice of a nonprofit tax adviser. For many nonprofit tax issues, the help of a tax adviser with specific expertise in and experience with IRS 501(c)(3) tax-exemption statutes and regulations is essential.

Consider the same factors for finding, choosing, using, and resolving problems with a tax professional as those discussed above for legal services. Shop around for someone recommended by other nonprofit people and organizations you respect. Again, you may be able to take advantage of the lower rates offered by newer local practitioners or a firm that is interested in your nonprofit mission. Your tax person should be available over the phone to answer routine questions or by email or fax to handle paperwork and correspondence with a minimum of formality or ritual. It is likely that you will spend much more time dealing with your tax adviser than your legal adviser, so be particularly attentive to the personal side of this relationship.

As with legal issues, it pays to learn as much as you can about nonprofit and employment taxation and forms. Not only will you have to buy less help from professionals, but you'll be in a good position to make good financial and tax-planning decisions. IRS forms and publications, nonprofit resource and law library publications, nonprofit consortiums, and other sources provide accessible information on nonprofit tax issues. For starters, visit the IRS website at www.irs.gov, and spend some time reading the materials and resources available on their "Charities & Non-Profits" section. ●

How to Use the CD-ROM

Please read this appendix and the ReadMe.txt file included on the CD-ROM for instructions on using it.

In accordance with U.S. copyright laws, the CD-ROM and its files are for your personal use only.

The CD-ROM can be used with Windows computers. It is not a standalone software program. It installs files that use software programs that need to be on your computer already.

Note to Macintosh users: This CD-ROM and its files should work on Macintosh computers. Please note, however, that Nolo cannot provide technical support for non-Windows users.

How to View the README File

To view the file ReadMe.txt, insert the CD-ROM into your computer's CD-ROM drive and follow these instructions:

Windows 2000, XP, and Vista
(1) On your computer's desktop, double click the My Computer icon; (2) double click the icon for the CD-ROM drive into which the CD-ROM was inserted; (3) double click the ReadMe.txt file.

Macintosh
(1) On your computer's desktop, double click the icon for the CD-ROM that you inserted and (2) double click the ReadMe.txt file.

Installing the Form Files Onto Your Computer

Before you can do anything with the files on the CD-ROM, you need to install them onto your computer.

Insert the CD-ROM and do the following.

Windows 2000, XP, and Vista

Follow the instructions that appear on the screen.

If nothing happens when you insert the CD-ROM, then (1) double click the My Computer icon; (2) double click the icon for the CD-ROM drive that you inserted the CD-ROM into; (3) double click the file Setup.exe.

Macintosh

If the Nonprofit Forms CD window is not open, open it by double clicking the Nonprofit Forms CD icon.

(1) Select the Nonprofit Forms folder icon and (2) drag and drop the folder icon onto your computer.

Where Are the Files Installed?

Windows 2000, XP, and Vista

RTF files are installed by default to the Nonprofit Forms subfolder of your computer's Program Files folder.

Macintosh

RTF files are located in the Nonprofit Forms folder.

Using the Word Processing Files to Create Documents

The CD-ROM includes word processing files that you can open, complete, print, and save with your word processing program. All word processing forms come in rich text format and have the extension ".rtf." For example, the Meeting Summary Sheet discussed in Chapter 3 is on the file Summary.rtf. RTF files can be read by most recent word processing programs including Microsoft *Word*, Windows *WordPad*, and recent versions of Corel *WordPerfect*.

The following are general instructions. Because each word processor uses different commands to open, format, save, and print documents, refer to your word processor's help file for specific instructions.

Do not call Nolo's technical support if you have questions on how to use your word processor or your computer.

Opening a File

You can open word processing files in any of the three following ways:

1. Windows users can open a file by selecting its "shortcut." (1) Click the Windows "Start" button; (2) open the Programs folder; (3) open the Nonprofit Forms folder; (4) click the shortcut to the form you want to work with.

2. Both Windows and Macintosh users can open a file by double clicking it. (1) Use My Computer or Windows Explorer (Windows 2000, XP, or Vista) or the Finder (Macintosh) to go to the Nonprofit Forms folder and (2) double click the file you want to open.

3. Windows and Macintosh users can open a file from within their word processor. (1) Open your word processor; (2) go to the File menu and choose the Open command. This opens a dialog box where (3) you will select the location and name of the file. (You will navigate to the version of the Nonprofit Forms folder that you've installed on your computer.)

Editing Your Document

Here are tips for working on your document.

Refer to the book's instructions and sample agreements for help.

Underlines indicate where to enter information, frequently including bracketed instructions. Delete the underlines and instructions before finishing your document.

Signature lines should appear on a page with at least some text from the document itself.

Editing Forms That Have Optional or Alternative Text

Some forms have check boxes that appear before text. Check boxes indicate:

- optional text that you can choose to include or exclude, or
- alternative text that you select to include, excluding the other alternatives.

Using the forms on the Forms CD, we recommend doing the following:

Optional text

Delete optional text you do not want to include and keep that which you do. In either case, delete the check box and the italicized instructions. If you choose to delete an optional numbered clause, renumber the subsequent clauses after deleting it.

Alternative text

Delete the alternatives that you do not want to include first. Then delete the remaining check boxes, as well as the italicized instructions that you need to select one of the alternatives provided.

Printing Out the Document

Use your word processor's or text editor's Print command to print out your document.

Saving Your Document

Use the Save As command to save and rename your document. You will be unable to use the Save command because the files are "read-only." If you save the file without renaming it, the underlines that indicate where you need to enter your information will be lost, and you will be unable to create a new document with this file without recopying the original file from the CD-ROM.

Forms on the CD-ROM

The following forms are in Rich Text Format (RTF):

Form Title	File Name
Membership Roster	Roster.rtf
Meeting Summary Sheet	Summary.rtf
Call of Meeting	CallMeeting.rtf
Meeting Participant List	Participants.rtf
Notice of Meeting	Notice.rtf
Waiver of Notice of Meeting	Waiver.rtf
Acknowledgment of Receipt of Notice of Meeting	Acknowledge.rtf
Proxy	Proxy.rtf
Approval of Minutes	MinuteOK.rtf
Minutes of the Annual Meeting of Directors	MinutesAnnualDir.rtf
Minutes of a Special Meeting of Directors	MinutesSpecialDir.rtf
Minutes of the Annual Meeting of Members	MinutesAnnualMem.rtf
Minutes of a Special Meeting of Members	MinutesSpecialMem.rtf
Written Consent to Action Without Meeting	Consent.rtf

Nonprofit Corporate Contact Information

Alabama

Corporate Filing Office

Secretary of State

www.sos.state.al.us/business/corporations.aspx

Nonprofit Corporation Law Online

The Alabama Nonprofit Act is contained in Title 10, Chapter 3A, of the Alabama statutes, and is browsable from the following website page (Select "Title 10," then "Chapter 3A"):

www.legislature.state.al.us/CodeofAlabama/1975/coatoc.htm

Alaska

Corporate Filing Office

Department of Commerce and Economic Development

www.commerce.state.ak.us/occ/home.htm

Nonprofit Corporation Law Online

The Alaska Nonprofit Corporation Act is contained in Title 10, Chapter 10.20, of the Alaska statutes (starting at Section 10.20.005) and can be browsed online. Go to the Web page listed below (the corporations section home page), select the link to "Alaska Statutes and Regulations," then select "The Current Alaska Statutes," expand the Title 10 heading and select "Chapter 10.20" to view the Nonprofit Corporation Act.

http://www.commerce.state.ak.us/occ/home.htm

Arizona

Corporate Filing Office

Arizona Corporation Commission

www.cc.state.az.us/corp/index.htm

Nonprofit Corporation Law Online

The Arizona Nonprofit Corporation Act is contained in Title 10, Chapter 24, of the Arizona Statutes, starting at Section 10.3101, and is browsable from the following website page (click "Title 10," then scroll down to "Chapter 24"):

http://www.azleg.gov/ArizonaRevisedStatutes.asp

Arkansas

Corporate Filing Office

Secretary of State

www.sosweb.state.ar.us/corp_ucc.html

Nonprofit Corporation Law Online

The 1993 Arkansas Nonprofit Corporation Act is located in Title 4 (Business and Commercial Law), Subtitle 3 (Corporations and Associations), Chapter 33, starting with Section 4-33-101, and is browsable from the following website page (first click "Arkansas Code," then select "Title 4," then "Subtitle 3," then "Chapter 33"):

www.arkleg.state.ar.us/Siteindex.asp?

California

Corporate Filing Office

Secretary of State

www.ss.ca.gov/business/business.htm

Nonprofit Corporation Law Online

The California Nonprofit Corporation Act is broken into three parts, with a separate part for public benefit, religious, and mutual benefit nonprofit corporations. The Nonprofit Public Benefit law starts at Section 5110 of the Corporations Code; the Nonprofit Religious Corporation Law starts at Section 9110; and the Nonprofit Mutual Benefit Law starts at Section 7110. To browse the law, go to the following website page (check the "Corporations Code" box, then click the search button at the bottom of the page; then scroll down to the section you wish to view):

www.leginfo.ca.gov/calaw.html

Colorado

Corporate Filing Office
Secretary of State

www.sos.state.co.us/pubs/business/main.htm

Nonprofit Corporation Law Online
The Colorado Revised Nonprofit Corporation Act is contained in Title 7, Articles 121 through 137, of the Colorado Statutes, starting with Section 7-121-101, and is browsable from the following website page (select "Colorado Statutes" (ignore the first "Corporations" heading), then "Nonprofit corporations," then select from the list of headings to browse sections of the BCA):

http://198.187.128.12/colorado/lpext.dll?f=templates&fn=fs-main.htm&2.0

Connecticut

Corporate Filing Office
Secretary of State

www.sots.ct.gov/CommercialRecording/Crdindex.html

Nonprofit Corporation Law Online
The Connecticut Revised Nonstock Corporation Act is contained in Title 33, Chapter 602, of the Connecticut Statutes, starting with Section 33-1000, and is browsable from the following website page (click, "Browse Statutes," then select "Title 33," then click "Chapter 602"):

http://www.cga.ct.gov/asp/menu/Statutes.asp

Delaware

Corporate Filing Office
Department of State

www.state.de.us/corp/default.shtml

Nonprofit Corporation Law Online

The Delaware General Corporation Law (nonprofit statutes are interspersed with regular for-profit corporation statutes) is contained in Title 8 (Corporations), Chapter 1, of the Delaware Statutes, starting with Section 101, and is browsable from the following website page (click "Delaware Laws Online" under Services, then click the "General Corporation Law" under Title 8, Chapter 1):

www.state.de.us/corp

District of Columbia

Corporate Filing Office

Department of Consumer & Regulatory Affairs

http://mblr.dc.gov/corp/index.shtm

Nonprofit Corporation Law Online

The DC Nonprofit Corporation Act is contained in Title 29 (Corporations), Chapter 3, of the DC Code, starting with Section 29-301.01, and is browsable from the following website page (select "District of Columbia," "District of Columbia Code," then "Division 5," then "Title 29," then "Chapter 3"):

http://www.michie.com

Florida

Corporate Filing Office

Department of State

www.dos.state.fl.us/doc/index.html

Nonprofit Corporation Law Online

The Florida Not For Profit Corporation Act is contained in Title XXXVI (Business Organizations), Chapter 617, of the Florida Statutes, starting with Section 617.01011, and is browsable from the following website page (click the "Statutes and Constitution" tab, then "Florida Statutes," then select "Title XXXVI," then "Chapter 617" from the index):

www.leg.state.fl.us/Welcome/index.cfm

Georgia

Corporate Filing Office

Secretary of State

www.sos.state.ga.us/corporations

Nonprofit Corporation Law Online

The Georgia Nonprofit Corporation Code starts with Section 14-3-101 of the Georgia Code, and is browsable from the following website page (expand "Title 14, then Chapter 3" to start browsing the Nonprofit Code—you may first be asked to acknowledge that you understand the terms of use before being granted free access to the Georgia Code, which is provided by the state of Georgia and LexisNexis):

http://w3.lexis-nexis.com/hottopics/gacode/Default.asp

Hawaii

Corporate Filing Office

Department of Commerce and Consumer Affairs

www.hawaii.gov/dcca/areas/breg

Nonprofit Corporation Law Online

The Hawaii Nonprofit Corporation Act is contained in Chapter 414D of the Hawaii Statutes, and is browsable from the following website page (enter the site; select "Legal Info" at the side of the page; click "Statutes"; then select "Hawaii Nonprofit Corporation Act"):

www.businessregistrations.com

Idaho

Corporate Filing Office

Secretary of State

www.idsos.state.id.us/corp/corindex.htm

Nonprofit Corporation Law Online

The Idaho Nonprofit Corporation Act is contained in Title 30, Chapter 3, of the Idaho Statutes, starting with Section 30-3-1, and is browsable from the following website page (click "Title 30," then "Chapter 3" to start browsing the Act):

http://www3.state.id.us/idstat/TOC/idstTOC.html

Illinois

Corporate Filing Office

Illinois Secretary of State

www.cyberdriveillinois.com/departments/business_services/home.html

Nonprofit Corporation Law Online

The Illinois General Not For Profit Corporation Act is contained in Chapter 805 (Business Organizations), starting with Section 180/105, and is browsable from the following website page (click "Chapter 805," then click "805 ILCS 105" to browse the Act):

http://www.ilga.gov/legislation/ilcs/ilcs.asp

Indiana

Corporate Filing Office

Secretary of State

www.in.gov/sos/business/corporations.html

Nonprofit Corporation Law Online

The Indiana Not For Profit Corporation Act is contained in Title 23 (Business and Other Associations), Article 17, of the Indiana Code, starting with Section 23-17-1-1, and is browsable from the following website page (select "Title 23," then "Article 17"):

www.in.gov/legislative/ic/code

Iowa

Corporate Filing Office
Secretary of State

www.state.ia.us/tax/index.html

Nonprofit Corporation Law Online
The Revised Iowa Nonprofit Corporation Act is contained in Title XII (Business Entities), Chapter 504, of the Iowa Code, starting with Section 504.101, and is browsable from the following website page: click "Tables and Index to the Code of Iowa" under the "2007 Iowa Code" heading, then click "Skeleton Index," then open the "2007 Iowa Code" folder in the left pane, then "Statutes," then select "Title XII Business Entities," then open the folder for Subtitle 5, then open the folder for "Chapter 504 Revised Iowa Nonprofit Corporation Act":

http://www.legis.state.ia.us/IowaLaw.html

Kansas

Corporate Filing Office
Kansas Secretary of State

www.kssos.org/main.html

Nonprofit Corporation Law Online
The Kansas corporate statutes are contained in Chapter 17 of the Kansas statutes, beginning with Article 60 (the profit and nonprofit statutes are consolidated together). In the box at the bottom of the page titled "Statute Table of Contents," select "Chapter 17" (use the arrow keys to navigate through the list), then click "Get Articles in Chapter." Select Article 60 to browse the corporate statutes:

www.kslegislature.org/cgi-bin/statutes/index.cgi

Kentucky

Corporate Filing Office
Secretary of State

http://sos.ky.gov/business

Nonprofit Corporation Law Online

The Kentucky nonprofit statutes are contained in Title XXIII (Private Corporations and Associations), Chapter 273, of the Kentucky Statutes, starting with Section 273.161, and are browsable from the following website page (select "Title XXIII, Chapter 273," then scroll to "Section .161" to begin browsing the nonprofit corporation statutes):

www.lrc.state.ky.us/krs/titles.htm

Louisiana

Corporate Filing Office

Secretary of State

www.sec.state.la.us/comm/corp/corp-index.htm

Nonprofit Corporation Law Online

The Louisiana Nonprofit Corporation Law is contained in Title XII Corporations and Associations, Chapter 2, of the Louisiana Revised Statutes, starting with Section 12:201. To start browsing the Act, click the "Louisiana Laws" link on the website page, www. legis.state.la.us. Use the topmost "Search by Specific Law Body" section of the page. Type "12" in the Title box, and "201" in the Section box.

www.legis.state.la.us

Maine

Corporate Filing Office

Secretary of State

www.state.me.us/sos/cec/corp/corp.htm

Nonprofit Corporation Law Online

The Maine Nonprofit Corporation Act is contained in Title 13B of the Maine Statutes, starting with Section 101, and is browsable from the following website page (select Title 13B):

http://janus.state.me.us/legis/statutes

Maryland

Corporate Filing Office

Department of Assessments & Taxation

www.dat.state.md.us/sdatweb/charter.html

Nonprofit Corporation Law Online

The Maryland General Corporation Law, Titles 1 through 3 of the Corporations and Associations Code of Maryland, covers both profit and nonprofit corporations unless a special provision of Title 5, Subtitle 2, of the Corporations and Associations Code provides otherwise. To browse Titles 1 through 3, and Title 5, Subtitle 2, go to the following website page (select Maryland, then click the Maryland Code folder, then the Corporations and Associations Code, then browse Titles 1 through 3 and Title 5, Subtitle 2. Also see Title 5, Subtitle 3, for special provisions that can apply to religious nonprofit corporations formed by churches):

www.michie.com

Massachusetts

Corporate Filing Office

Corporations Division

www.sec.state.ma.us/cor/coridx.htm

Nonprofit Corporation Law Online

The Massachusetts Nonprofit Corporation Act is contained in Chapter 180 of the Massachusetts General Laws, and is browsable from the following website page (select "General Laws," then select "Link to a Specific Chapter or Section," then type "180" in the Chapter No. box, leave the section number field empty, and click "get Link"; then browse specific section from the list of links). Nonprofit corporations also are subject to general provisions of the Business Corporation Law contained in Chapter 156B of the Laws:

www.state.ma.us/legis/legis.htm

Michigan

Corporate Filing Office
Bureau of Commercial Services

www.michigan.gov/cis

Nonprofit Corporation Law Online
The Michigan Nonprofit Corporation Act is contained in Chapter 450 (Corporations) of the Michigan Compiled laws, starting with Section 450.2101, and is browsable from the following website page (select "Chapter Index" under "Laws" in the left pane, then select "Chapter 450," then scroll down and select "Act 162 of 1982—Nonprofit Corporation Act" at the bottom of the page):

www.michiganlegislature.org

Minnesota

Corporate Filing Office
Secretary of State

http://www.sos.state.mn.us/home/index.asp

Nonprofit Corporation Law Online
The Minnesota Nonprofit Corporation Act is contained in Chapter 317A of the Minnesota Statutes, starting with Section 317A.001, and is browsable from the following website page (select "Chapter 300 through 319B," then select "Chapter 317A"):

http://ros.leg.mn/revisor/pages/statute/statute_toc.php

Mississippi

Corporate Filing Office
Secretary of State

www.sos.state.ms.us/busserv/corp/jer_corporations.asp

Nonprofit Corporation Law Online

The Mississippi Nonprofit Corporation Act is contained in the Title 79 (Corporations, Associations and Partnerships) of the Mississippi Code, Chapter 11, starting with Section 79-11-101, and is browsable from the following website page (select "Mississippi," open the "Mississippi Code" folder, then the "Title 79" folder, then the "Chapter 11" folder, then the "Mississippi Nonprofit Corporation Act" folder):

www.michie.com

Missouri

Corporate Filing Office

Secretary of State

www.sos.mo.gov/business/corporations/Default.asp

Nonprofit Corporation Law Online

The Missouri Nonprofit Corporation Act is contained in Title XXIII (Corporations, Associations and Partnerships) of the Missouri Statutes, Chapter 355, starting with Section 355.001, and is browsable from the following website page:

www.moga.state.mo.us/statutes/c355.htm

Montana

Corporate Filing Office

Secretary of State

http://sos.state.mt.us/BSB/index.asp

Nonprofit Corporation Law Online

The Montana Nonprofit Corporation Act is contained in Title 35 (Corporations, Partnerships and Associations) of the Montana Code, Chapter 2, starting with Section 35-2-113, and is browsable from the following website page (select "Title 35," then "Chapter 2," then "Part 1," then scroll down to start browsing at "Section 113"):

http://data.opi.state.mt.us/bills/mca_toc/index.htm

Nebraska

Corporate Filing Office
Secretary of State

www.sos.state.ne.us/business/corp_serv

Nonprofit Corporation Law Online
The Nebraska Nonprofit Corporation Act is contained in Chapter 21 (Corporations and Other Companies) of the Nebraska Statutes, starting with Section 21-1901, and is browsable from the website page listed below. Click the "Statutes" tab, select Chapter "21," then scroll down to Section 21-1901 to begin browsing the Nonprofit Corporation Act):

http://uniweb.legislature.ne.gov/legaldocs/search.php

Nevada

Corporate Filing Office
Secretary of State

www.sos.state.nv.us/comm_rec/index.htm

Nonprofit Corporation Law Online
The Nevada Nonprofit Corporation Act is contained in Title 7 (Business Associations; Securities; Commodities), Chapter 82, of the Nevada Statutes, starting with Section 82.006. You can browse it from the following website page (select the "Table of Contents to the Nevada Revised Statutes" from the submenu that appears from the "Law Library" item in the left panel, then select "Title 7, Chapter 82"):

www.leg.state.nv.us

New Hampshire

Corporate Filing Office
Secretary of State

www.sos.nh.gov/corporate

Nonprofit Corporation Law Online

The New Hampshire nonprofit corporation laws are contained in Title XXVII (Voluntary Corporations and Associations), Chapter 292, of the New Hampshire Statutes, starting with Section 292:1, and is browsable from the website page listed below (select "Form & Laws" in the left pane, then select "Non Profits," then select "State of New Hampshire Revised Statutes Online, Voluntary Corporations & Associations (Chapter 292)"):

www.sos.nh.gov/corporate

New Jersey

Corporate Filing Office

Department of Treasury

www.state.nj.us/njbgs

Nonprofit Corporation Law Online

The New Jersey Nonprofit Corporation Act is contained in Title 15A of the New Jersey Statutes, starting with Section 15A:1-1, and is browsable from the following website page (select "Statutes," then select "Browse by Table of Contents," then select Title 15A):

www.njleg.state.nj.us

New Mexico

Corporate Filing Office

Public Regulation Commission

www.nmprc.state.nm.us/cb.htm

Nonprofit Corporation Law Online

The New Mexico Nonprofit Corporation Act is contained in Chapter 53 (Corporations), Article 8, of the New Mexico Statutes, starting with Section 53-8-1, and is browsable from the following website page (first select "Statutes" in the left panel, then, in the left panel select "New Mexico Statutes and Court Rules," then the folder titled "Statutory Chapters in New Mexico Statutes Annotated 1978," then scroll down in the left panel and open the Chapter 53 folder, then open the Article 8 folder and select sections of the Act to browse):

http://legis.state.nm.us

New York

Corporate Filing Office

Department of State

www.dos.state.ny.us/corp/corpwww.html

Nonprofit Corporation Law Online

The New York Not For Profit Corporation Law is contained in Chapter 35 of the New York Consolidated Laws, starting with Section 101, and is browsable from the following website page (click "New York State Laws," then "New York State Consolidated Laws," then "Not For Profit Corporation," then select article headings to view each part of the law):

http://assembly.state.ny.us/leg

North Carolina

Corporate Filing Office

Department of the Secretary of State

www.secretary.state.nc.us/corporations

Nonprofit Corporation Law Online

The North Carolina Nonprofit Corporation Act is contained in Chapter 55A of the North Carolina Statutes, starting with Section 55A-1-01, and can be browsed at the website page shown below (click "NC General Statutes" at the bottom of the page, then click "Browse Table of Contents" in the right pane, then select "Chapter 55A, North Carolina Nonprofit Corporation Act"; also note that name and registered agent requirements for all types of corporations are contained in Chapter 55D of the NC General Statutes):

www.secstate.state.nc.us

North Dakota

Corporate Filing Office
Secretary of State

www.nd.gov/sos/businessserv

Nonprofit Corporation Law Online
The North Dakota Nonprofit Corporation Act is contained in Title 10-33 of the North Dakota Century Code, starting with Section 10-33-01, and is browsable from the website page listed below (select "State Laws," then click "ND Century Code" in the left pane, then click "10 Corporations," then select the "Chapter 10-33" to browse sections of the Nonprofit Corporation Act):

www.legis.nd.gov

Ohio

Corporate Filing Office
Secretary of State

www.sos.state.oh.us/sos/businessservices/corp.aspx

Nonprofit Corporation Law Online
The Ohio Nonprofit Corporation Law is contained in Title XVII (Corporations-Partnerships), Chapter 1702, of the Ohio Statutes, starting with Section 1702.01, and is browsable from the following website page (click "Revised Code," select "Title 17" in the left pane, click "Chapter 1702," then select each section of the law you wish to view):

http://onlinedocs.andersonpublishing.com

Oklahoma

Corporate Filing Office
Secretary of State

www.sos.state.ok.us/business/business_filing.htm

Nonprofit Corporation Law Online

The Oklahoma nonprofit corporation statutes are consolidated with the profit corporation statutes in the Oklahoma General Corporation Act contained in Title 18 of Oklahoma Statutes, starting with Section 18-1001. The GCA is browsable from the website page listed below. Select "Link to Statutes" in the left panel, then click "Expand" for Title 18, then scroll down to Section 1001 to the start of the General Corporation Act.

www.sos.state.ok.us/exec_legis/exec_leg_home.htm

Oregon

Corporate Filing Office

Secretary of State

www.filinginoregon.com

Nonprofit Corporation Law Online

The Oregon Nonprofit Corporation Act is contained in Chapter 65 of the Oregon Statutes, starting with Section 65.001, and is browsable from the following website page:

www.leg.state.or.us/ors/065.html

Pennsylvania

Corporate Filing Office

Department of State

www.dos.state.pa.us/corps/site/default.asp

Nonprofit Corporation Law Online

The Pennsylvania Nonprofit Corporation Law of 1988 is contained in Title 15 of the Pennsylvania Statutes, starting with Section 5101. While state rules (contained in a state code) are provided on the link shown below (see Chapter 25 for Nonstock Corporation guidelines and rules), the statutes are not provided online at this time.

www.pacode.com/secure/data/019/019toc.html

Rhode Island

Corporate Filing Office

Secretary of State

www3.sec.state.ri.us/divs/corps

Nonprofit Corporation Law Online

The Rhode Island Nonprofit Corporation Act is contained in Title 7 (Corporations, Associations and Partnerships), Chapter 7-6, of the Rhode Island General Laws, starting with Section 7-6-1, and is browsable from the following website page (select Chapter 7-6 from the Index):

www.rilin.state.ri.us/statutes/title7/index.htm

South Carolina

Corporate Filing Office

Secretary of State

www.scsos.com/Corporations.htm

Nonprofit Corporation Law Online

The South Carolina Nonprofit Corporation Act is contained in Title 33 (Corporations, Partnerships and Associations), Chapter 31, of the South Carolina Code, starting with Section 33-31-101, and is browsable from the website page listed below (select Title 33, then scroll down and select "SOUTH CAROLINA NONPROFIT CORPORATION ACT (t33c031)"):

www.scstatehouse.net/code/statmast.htm

South Dakota

Corporate Filing Office

Secretary of State

www.sdsos.gov/busineservices/corporations.shtm

Nonprofit Corporation Law Online

The South Dakota Nonprofit Corporation Act, contained in Title 47 (Corporations), starting with Chapter 22 of the South Dakota Codified Laws, is browsable from the following website page (select South Dakota, then drill down through the folder headings in the left pane, as follows: "South Dakota Codified Laws," "Title 47," "Chapter 47-22"):

www.michie.com

Tennessee

Corporate Filing Office

Department of State

www.state.tn.us/sos/bus-svc/corporations.htm

Nonprofit Corporation Law Online

The Tennessee Nonprofit Corporation Act is contained in Title 48 (Corporations and Associations), Chapters 51 through 68, starting with Section 48-51-101 of the Tennessee Code, and is browsable from the following website page (select Tennessee, then drill down through the folder headings in the left pane, as follows: "Tennessee Code," "Title 48," "Chapter 51" to view the first chapter of the Nonprofit Corporation Act—select other chapters to continue browsing the remaining sections of the Act):

www.michie.com

Texas

Corporate Filing Office

Secretary of State

www.sos.state.tx.us/corp/index.shtml

Nonprofit Corporation Law Online

A Texas nonprofit corporation is governed by Titles 1 and 2 of the Texas Business Organizations Code (BOC). Specific nonprofit provisions are contained in Chapter 22 of Title 2. These provisions can be browsed from the following URL:

http://tlo2.tlc.state.tx.us/statutes/bo.toc.htm

Utah

Corporate Filing Office

Division of Corporations and Commercial Code

http://corporations.utah.gov/index.html

Nonprofit Corporation Law Online

The Utah Revised Nonprofit Corporation Act is contained in Title 16, Chapter 6a, of the Utah Code, starting with Section 16-6a-101, and is browsable from the website page listed below (select search by "Keyword," then expand the left pane index to select Title 16, Chapter 6a):

www.le.state.ut.us/documents/code_const.htm

Vermont

Corporate Filing Office

Secretary of State

www.sec.state.vt.us/corps/corpindex.htm

Nonprofit Corporation Law Online

The Vermont Nonprofit Corporation Act is contained in Title 11B of the Vermont Statutes, and is browsable from the following website page (select "Vermont Statutes," then "Title 11B"):

www.leg.state.vt.us

Virginia

Corporate Filing Office

Clerk of the State Corporation Commission

www.scc.virginia.gov/division/clk/index.htm

Nonprofit Corporation Law Online

The Virginia Nonstock Corporation Act is contained in Title 13.1 (Corporations) of the Virginia Code, Chapter 10, starting with Section 13.1-801, and is browsable from the following website page (click "Code of Virginia," then click "Table of Contents" on the search page; then select Title 13.1, then click Chapter 10 to see a list of the sections in the Act):

http://legis.state.va.us/codecomm/codehome.htm

Washington

Corporate Filing Office

Secretary of State

www.secstate.wa.gov/corps

Nonprofit Corporation Law Online

The Washington Nonprofit Corporation Act is contained in Title 24 of the Washington Code, starting with Section 24.03.005, and is browsable from the following website page (click "Revised Code of Washington (RCW)," then select "Title 24," then "Chapter 24.03"):

www1.leg.wa.gov/CodeReviser

West Virginia

Corporate Filing Office

Secretary of State

www.wvsos.com

Nonprofit Corporation Law Online

The West Virginia Nonprofit Corporation Act is contained in Chapter 31E, of the West Virginia Code, beginning with Section 31E-1-101a, and is browsable from the following website page (select "WV Code" at the top of the page, then select "WV Nonprofit Corporations"):

www.wvsos.com/business

Wisconsin

Corporate Filing Office

Department of Financial Institutions

www.wdfi.org/corporations

Nonprofit Corporation Law Online

The Wisconsin Nonprofit Corporation Act is contained in Chapter 181 of the Wisconsin Statutes, starting with Section 181.0103, and is browsable from the following website page (select "Statutes & Rules" on the left panel, then select "Nonstock Corporation"):

www.wdfi.org/corporations/default.htm

Wyoming

Corporate Filing Office

Secretary of State

http://soswy.state.wy.us/corporat/corporat.htm

Nonprofit Corporation Law Online

The Wyoming Nonprofit Corporation Act is contained in Title 17 of the Wyoming Statutes, Chapter 19, starting with section 17-19-101, and is browsable from the following website page (click the link to the "Nonprofit Corporation Act"; for special provisions that apply to churches, click "Churches and Religious Societies Generally"):

http://soswy.state.wy.us/corporat/statutes.htm ●

Meeting and Minutes Forms

Membership Roster

Certificate Number	Type or Class of Membership (Voting, Nonvoting, Sponsor, etc.)	Date of Issuance	Member's Name and Address	Date of Termination

Meeting Summary Sheet

Name of Nonprofit: _____

Year: _____

Type of Meeting: ☐ Annual/Regular   ☐ Special

Meeting of: ☐ Directors   ☐ Members

☐ _____ Committee

Date: _____ Time: _____

Location: _____

Meeting Called By: _____

Purpose: _____

Committee or Other Reports or Presentations: _____

_____

Other Reminders or Notes: _____

_____

_____

Notice Required: ☐ Written   ☐ Verbal   ☐ Not Required

Notice Must Be Given by Date: _____

Notice of Meeting Given To:

Name	Type of Notice*	Location or Phone Number	Date Notice Given	Date Acknowledged Receipt

* **Types of Notice:** written (mailed, hand-delivered), verbal (in-person, telephone conversation, answering machine, voice mail), email, fax.

Call of Meeting

To:

Secretary: _____

Name of nonprofit: _____

Address of nonprofit: _____

_____

The following person(s):

Name _____ Title _____

_____ _____

_____ _____

authorized under provisions of the bylaws of _____ ,

hereby make(s) a call and request to hold a(n) _____

meeting of the _____ of the corporation for the purpose(s) of:

_____ .

The date and time of the meeting requested is: _____ .

The requested location for the meeting is: _____ ,

state of _____ .

The secretary is requested to provide all proper notices as required by the bylaws
of the corporation and any other necessary materials to all persons entitled to
attend the meeting.

Date: _____

Signed: _____

Meeting Participant List

Name of Nonprofit: _____

Type of Meeting: ☐ Annual/Regular ☐ Special

Meeting of: ☐ Directors ☐ Members

☐ _____ Committee

Date: _____

Meeting Participants (list names in alphabetical order):

Name: _____

Address: _____

Telephone: _____

☐ Director

☐ Member: Type of Membership and Number of Votes: _____

☐ Committee Member

☐ Officer: Title _____

☐ Other (position and reason for attendance): _____

_____

Name: _____

Address: _____

Telephone: _____

☐ Director

☐ Member: Type of Membership and Number of Votes: _____

☐ Committee Member

☐ Officer: Title _____

☐ Other (position and reason for attendance): _____

_____

Notice of Meeting

of

_____

A(n) _____ meeting of the _____

of _____ will be held at

_____ ,

state of _____ , on _____ , 20_____

at _____ : _____ __ m.

The purpose(s) of the meeting is/are as follows: _____

_____

_____ .

[_Optional—For membership proxy organizations only._] If you are a member and cannot attend the meeting and wish to designate another person to vote your membership for you, please deliver a signed membership proxy form to the secretary of the corporation before the meeting. Contact the secretary if you need help obtaining or preparing this form.

Signature of Secretary: _____

Name of Secretary: _____

Nonprofit corporation: _____

Address: _____

_____ .

Phone: _____ Fax: _____

Waiver of Notice of Meeting

of

_____

The undersigned _____ hereby waive notice of

and consent to the holding of the _____ meeting of

the _____ of _____ held

at _____ ,

state of _____ , on _____ , 20 _____

at _____ : _____ _____ m. for the purposes of: _____

_____ .

Dated: _____

Signature _____ Printed Name _____

_____ _____

_____ _____

_____ _____

_____ _____

_____ _____

_____ _____

Acknowledgment of Receipt of Notice of Meeting

I received notice of a(n) _____ meeting of the

_____ of _____ on

_____ , _____ . The notice of meeting stated the date, time,

place, and purpose of the upcoming meeting.

The notice of meeting was:

☐ received by fax

☐ delivered orally to me in person

☐ delivered orally to me by phone call

☐ left in a message on an answering machine or voice mail

☐ delivered by mail

☐ delivered via email

☐ other: _____

Dated: _____

Signed: _____

Printed Name: _____

Please return to:

Name: _____

Nonprofit corporation: _____

Address: _____

Phone: _____ Fax: _____

Proxy

The undersigned member of _____ authorizes

_____ to act as his/her proxy and

to represent and vote his/her membership at a(n) _____

meeting of members to be held at _____ ,

state of _____ , on _____ , _____

at _____ : _____ ___ m.

Dated: _____ _____

Signed: _____

Printed Name: _____

Please return proxy by _____ , _____ **to:**

Name: _____

Title: _____

Nonprofit corporation: _____

Address: _____

City, State, Zip: _____

Phone: _____ Fax: _____

Approval of Minutes

of

_____

The undersigned _____ consents to the minutes of

the _____ meeting of the _____

of _____ held at _____

_____ , state of _____ ,

on _____ , _____ at _____ : _____ ___ .m.,

attached to this form, and accept(s) the resolutions passed and decisions made at

such meeting as valid and binding acts of the _____

of the corporation.

Dated: _____

Signature: _____

Printed Name: _____

Minutes of the Annual Meeting of Directors of

_____

Date: _____

Location: _____

_____ acted as chairperson, and
_____ acted as secretary of the meeting.

The meeting was called to order at _____ : _____ ___ .m.

The secretary announced that the meeting was held pursuant to notice properly given or that notice had been waived by directors entitled to receive notice.

The secretary announced that the following directors, constituting a quorum, were present at the meeting:

Present in person:

_____ , _____ , _____ .

_____ , _____ , _____ .

_____ , _____ , _____ .

Present by conference call:

_____ , _____ , _____ .

Absent:

_____ , _____ , _____ .

The following persons were also present at the meeting:

Name	Title
_____	_____
_____	_____
_____	_____

Proceedings:

Election of Directors:

The following persons were elected directors of the corporation to serve a _____ year term.

_____ , _____ , _____

_____ , _____ , _____

_____ , _____ , _____ ,

_____ , _____ , _____ .

[*or*]

The following directors, having been elected to serve on the board for another _____ term by the members at an annual meeting of members held on _____ , _____ , accepted their positions on the board:

_____ , _____ , _____

_____ , _____ , _____

_____ , _____ , _____

_____ , _____ , _____ .

The secretary announced that the presence of the directors, including the newly elected directors, represented a quorum.

The minutes from the prior directors' meeting dated _____ , _____

☐ were read by the secretary.

☐ had been distributed prior to the meeting and a reading was dispensed with.

After discussion, a motion to approve the minutes was made by _____ ; seconded and approved.

The next item of business was the appointment of committee members and others to positions in service to the corporation. After discussion, the following persons were appointed to serve on the following committees or in the service of the corporation in other capacities for the term indicated below:

Name   Committee or Role   Term

_____   _____   _____

_____   _____   _____

_____   _____   _____

_____   _____   _____

_____   _____   _____

_____   _____   _____

_____   _____   _____

The following reports were presented:

Report: _____

_____

Report: _____

_____

Other Business:

_____

_____

_____

_____

_____

On motion duly made and passed, the following resolutions were adopted or rejected by the votes indicated below:

_____

_____

_____

_____ .

Future Business:

_____

_____

_____

_____ .

There being no further business to come before the meeting, the meeting was adjourned at _____ : _____ ___ .m.

_____

_____ , Secretary

Minutes of Special Meeting of Directors

of

_____

Date: _____

Location: _____

Purpose of meeting: _____
_____.

_____ acted as chairperson, and
_____ acted as secretary of the meeting.

The meeting was called to order at _____ : _____ __.m.

The secretary announced that the meeting was called by _____ ;
and that it was held pursuant to notice properly given or that notice had been
waived by directors entitled to receive notice.

The secretary announced that the following directors, constituting a quorum,
were present at the meeting:

Present in person:

_____ , _____ , _____

_____ , _____ , _____

_____ , _____ , _____

_____ , _____ , _____ .

Present by conference call:

_____ , _____ , _____ .

Absent:

_____ , _____ , _____ .

The following persons were also present at the meeting:

Name _____ Title _____

_____ _____

_____ _____

_____ _____

Proceedings:

The chairperson called the meeting to order at _____ : _____ __ m.

The minutes from the prior directors' meeting dated _____ , _____

☐ were read by the secretary.

☐ had been distributed prior to the meeting and a reading was dispensed with.

After discussion, a motion to approve the minutes was made by _____
_____ ; seconded, and approved.

The following reports were presented:

Report: _____

_____

Report: _____

_____

Other Business:

_____

_____

_____

_____

On motion duly made and passed, the following resolutions were adopted or rejected by the votes indicated below:

_____

_____

_____

_____ .

Future Business:

_____

_____

_____

_____ .

There being no further business to come before the meeting, the meeting was adjourned at _____ : _____ ___ m.

_____

_____, Secretary

Minutes of Annual Meeting of Members

of

_____

Date: _____

Location: _____

Purpose: To elect directors and for the transaction of any other business that may properly come before the meeting, including _____ .

_____ acted as chairperson, and _____ acted as secretary of the meeting.

The meeting was called to order at _____ : _____ __ m.

The secretary announced that the meeting was called by _____ .

The secretary announced that the meeting was held pursuant to notice properly given or that notice had been waived by all members entitled to receive notice.

The secretary announced that an alphabetical list of the names and, if appropriate, type of membership interests held by all members of the nonprofit corporation was available and open to inspection by any person in attendance at the meeting.

Proceedings:

The secretary announced that the following members, constituting a quorum, were present in person or by proxy:

Name	Proxyholder, if any
_____	_____
_____	_____
_____	_____
_____	_____

The secretary attached written proxy statements, executed by the appropriate members, to these minutes for any members listed above represented by a proxyholder.

The following persons were also present at the meeting:

Name _____   Title _____

_____   _____

_____   _____

_____   _____

The minutes from the prior members' meeting dated _____ , _____

☐ were read by the secretary.

☐ had been distributed prior to the meeting and a reading was dispensed with.

After discussion, a motion to approve the minutes was made by _____

_____ ; seconded, and approved.

Election of Directors

The chairperson announced that the next item of business was the nomination and election of the board of directors for another _____ term of office. The following nominations were made and seconded:

Names of Nominees _____

_____

_____

_____

_____

_____

_____

_____

_____

The secretary next took the votes of members entitled to vote for the election of directors at the meeting. After counting the votes, the secretary announced that the following persons were elected to serve on the board of directors of this corporation for another term:

Name _____ Term _____

_____ _____

_____ _____

_____ _____

_____ _____

_____ _____

_____ _____

The following reports were presented:

Report: _____

_____

Report: _____

_____

Other Business:

_____

_____

_____

_____

_____

On motion duly made and passed, the following resolutions were adopted or rejected by the votes of members present in person or by proxy as indicated below:

_____

_____

_____

_____ .

There being no further business to come before the meeting, the meeting was adjourned at _____ : _____ ___ m.

_____

_____ , Secretary

Minutes of Special Meeting of Members

of

_____

Date: _____

Location: _____

Purpose of meeting: _____

_____

_____ acted as chairperson, and

_____ acted as secretary of the meeting.

The meeting was called to order at _____ : _____ __ m.

The secretary announced that the meeting was called by _____ ;
and that it was held pursuant to notice properly given or that notice had been
waived by members entitled to receive notice.

The secretary announced that an alphabetical list of the names and, if appropriate,
type of membership interest, held by all members of the corporation was
available and open to inspection by any person in attendance at the meeting.

The secretary announced that there were present, in person or by proxy,
representing a quorum of the members, the following members:

Name	Proxyholder, if any

The secretary attached written proxy statements, executed by the appropriate members, to these minutes for any members listed above represented by a proxyholder.

The following persons were also present at the meeting:

Name	Title

Proceedings:

The minutes from the prior members' meeting dated _____ , _____

☐ were read by the secretary.

☐ had been distributed prior to the meeting and a reading was dispensed with.

After discussion, a motion to approve the minutes was made by _____ _____ ; seconded, and approved.

The following reports were presented:

Report: _____

_____

Report: _____

_____

Other Business:

_____

_____

_____

_____

_____

On motion duly made and passed, the following resolutions were adopted or rejected by the votes of members present in person or by proxy as indicated below:

_____

_____

_____

_____

_____

_____

_____

_____

_____

_____ .

There being no further business to come before the meeting, the meeting was adjourned at _____ : _____ __ m.

_____

_____ , Secretary

Written Consent to Action Without Meeting

The undersigned _____ of _____
hereby consent as follows:

_____

_____

_____

_____

_____

_____

_____ .

Dated: _____

Signature: _____   Printed Name _____

_____   _____

_____   _____

_____   _____

_____   _____

_____   _____

_____   _____

_____   _____

_____   _____

_____   _____

Index

Get the Latest in the Law

 Nolo's Legal Updater
We'll send you an email whenever a new edition of your book is published!
Sign up at **www.nolo.com/legalupdater**.

 Updates at Nolo.com
Check **www.nolo.com/update** to find recent changes in the law that
affect the current edition of your book.

 Nolo Customer Service
To make sure that this edition of the book is the most recent one, call us at
800-728-3555 and ask one of our friendly customer service representatives
(7:00 am to 6:00 pm PST, weekdays only). Or find out at **www.nolo.com**.

 Complete the Registration & Comment Card ...
... and we'll do the work for you! Just indicate your preferences below:

Registration & Comment Card

NAME _____ DATE _____

ADDRESS _____

CITY _____ STATE _____ ZIP _____

PHONE _____ EMAIL _____

COMMENTS _____

WAS THIS BOOK EASY TO USE?   (VERY EASY)   5   4   3   2   1   (VERY DIFFICULT)

☐ Yes, you can quote me in future Nolo promotional materials. *Please include phone number above.*

☐ Yes, send me **Nolo's Legal Updater** via email when a new edition of this book is available.

Yes, I want to sign up for the following email newsletters:

  ☐ **NoloBriefs** (monthly)
  ☐ **Nolo's Special Offer** (monthly)
  ☐ **Nolo's BizBriefs** (monthly)
  ☐ **Every Landlord's Quarterly** (four times a year)

☐ Yes, you can give my contact info to carefully selected
   partners whose products may be of interest to me.

NORM1

Send to: **Nolo** 950 Parker Street Berkeley, CA 94710-9867, Fax: (800) 645-0895, or include all of
         the above information in an email to regcard@nolo.com with the subject line "NORM1."